Archibald M'Alpine Taylor

Boyhood hours

comprising a collection of simple poems, songs and odes

Archibald M'Alpine Taylor

Boyhood hours

comprising a collection of simple poems, songs and odes

ISBN/EAN: 9783337374426

Printed in Europe, USA, Canada, Australia, Japan

Cover: Foto ©Thomas Meinert / pixelio.de

More available books at **www.hansebooks.com**

BOYHOOD HOURS;

COMPRISING

A COLLECTION OF

SIMPLE POEMS, SONGS AND ODES.

BY

ARCHIBALD M'ALPINE TAYLOR.

𝔗𝔬𝔯𝔬𝔫𝔱𝔬:
HUNTER, ROSE AND COMPANY.
1881.
E.V.

ENTERED according to Act of the Parliament of Canada, in the year one thousand eight hundred and eighty-one, by ARCHIBALD M'ALPINE TAYLOR, in the office of the Minister of Agriculture.

CONTENTS.

	PAGE
Welcome	9
Mabel	12
Spes Gloriæ	47
Long ago	49
Love's Glorification—Dedicated to M——	50
The Children	53
Love's Legend	55
The Sailors' Prayer	58
Pride	60
To One I Love	62
The Summer Sabbath Morn	62
Or Ever	64
A Student's Thought	65
Spring in the Heart	76
A Student's Death	76
To a Lady Weeping	78
Sailor's Grave	79
Hector and Alice	81
Canadian Hymn	101
Song of the Cradle	101
"Good-bye": In Three Parts	104
A Song	106
To M——	107
She is Sleeping	107
The Truant-Player's Sister	108
Life	110
Inconstancy	111
On the Death of a Friend	113
To an Idiot Child	114

CONTENTS.

	PAGE
Love and Autumn	115
Beware	117
Genius	119
Youth, Love and the Grave	121
To A——	123
Morn	124
Stemming the Stream	124
Canada's Sons to their Sires	125
A Lesson	128
To an Old Maid	129
For a Little Girl's Album	130
Lines Suggested by the Death of W. C. Bryant	131
Thy Brother	135
The Sea by Moonlight	135
Love's Offering—A Flower	136
The Soldier-Boy	138
The Lost Hope	139
Thomas Carlyle: In Memoriam	140
Nature's Echoes	146
Daughters of the West	147
Sorrow	149
A Thought	150
To a Kind Friend	150
Lost	152
Marriage Hymn	153
A Tribute	154
The Old Teacher	155
The Song of Bobbie Burns	161
It May not Be	162
The Light, the Truth, the Way	163
A Thought	163
Battle Hymn	164
In Vain	166
Loyalty and War	167
To a Would-be Suicide	175

INTRODUCTION.

> "The proudest peer in all the realm
> Shall not wear head upon his shoulders
> Unless he pay me tribute."—HENRY vi.

THE intense spirit of toleration and liberal sentiment pervading the age is my chief plea for the publication of my little book.

Trusting more to the mercy and considerateness of the reading people, than to any meritoriousness of my work, I indulge the hope that honest effort, however mediocre its result, may command their commendation rather than their censure. In doffing my hat to the world I fear it may discover my baldness.

It must not be expected that the poetic productions of any native Canadian can, with justice, be compared with those of such masters of the lyre as Tennyson or Swinburne, Longfellow or Holmes, not to speak of the multitude of older masters; for, in this country poetry has not yet received the recognition of an art, and, although the native poetic element may be as rich as that of older countries, Canadian poetry must, for some time, lack much of that exquisite elegance of diction, and perfect polish of construction characteristic of enlightened art; nor should it, I think, be expected that the immature efforts of a puerile pen should be judged in the light of Canadian poetry advanced beyond the transition period, and impressed with the fixed individuality of genius; for it must be conceded that, even in young Canada, we have poets of which any nation might feel proud. I will be pardoned, I trust, for stating that during the few years of which every leisure moment has been devoted to the writing of these poems, I have, amidst many difficulties and disadvantages, for which, I am alike thankful to Providence and humanity, endeavored to keep faith with my profession both in preparation and practice. What I might achieve under more propitious circumstances, it would, on my part, be imprudent to conjecture; nor can I any more promise unswerving allegiance to the olive-crowned muse in the future, than I have given in the past; for I am only yet in the heat of a battle which I must wage, even though I may not win. But one thing I can, and do promise, that by whatever circumstances I shall be surrounded, *I shall always do my best;* and should there be but little sunshine I will the better improve that little.

It is interesting to observe that, among the arts, poetry is the only one left entirely to the care of the gods. The aspiring musician, painter or sculptor can, without difficulty, secure the requisite art education under competent masters, while the young poet, without aid or encouragement, must, led by the instinct of taste, preserve faithfulness to both nature and art, or wither under the lash of public criticism until experience makes him wise. The public, however, is not often too severe, and it is in anticipation of this "pleasing fear" I make my first literary adventure, hoping fully and profitably to appreciate the candid criticism of the world. Should the poems merit reading, I shall be greatly pleased; should they be worthy of criticism, I shall be delighted; should a small measure of approval greet them, I shall feel greatly encouraged; and only should they provoke ridicule, shall I feel slightly disappointed and hopelessly discouraged.

> "Here's freedom to him that wad read,
> Here's freedom to him that wad write!
> There's nane ever feared that the truth should be heard,
> But they wham the truth wad indict."—BURNS.

A. M. TAYLOR.

CLINTON, August 23rd, 1831.

BOYHOOD HOURS.

WELCOME.*

Hail! princely scion of that noble name,
Whose members died to build their country's fame,
Whose broadswords gleam'd in majesty and might,
Who lived for freedom,—died for Truth and Right!
Thou gallant son of such immortal sires,
Bred from their loins, and nurtured by their fires,
With pride in thee, thy country's raptured strain,
From its warm bosom, o'er Atlanta's main,
Far as the breakers of the frozen North,
Pours forth its praises of exalted worth.
Behold how every leaf in Scotia's vales
Breathes out sweet echoes to the sighing gales,
To bless some mem'ry of thy lineage old
Or shout of valor that hath ne'er been told.
Breathe on, sweet vales, and heather-crowned hills;
Your liquid warblings sing, ye rippling rills;
Ye thronging crowds, that say, adieu, in tears,
Still louder shout, till we can hear thy cheers,—
Till our broad land to its remotest bound,
Shall wake its music to the thrilling sound;—

---

* Written and published on the arrival of the Marquis and Princess in Canada.

Till the dark oceans of the east and west
Shall sing for glory o'er Kanatia's breast,—
Till every tongue shall be a patriot lyre,
And every heart becomes a patriot fire!
For thee the muse of wild Canadian song
Stands lonely waiting, 'midst the varied throng,
Sparkled her sandals with the morning dew;
Her garments, rustic, of the leaves that grew
Fast by dark stream with ivy mantled red;
A halo of bright cressets on her head;
Upon her brow, Hope's pure and twinkling star
Spreads its white lustre o'er the waves afar;
Her right hand waves the flag of victory;
Her left, subdues the chiding of the sea,
Long hath she strode, with patient hope imbued,
The silent kingdoms of the trackless wood,
Seeking a heart, her pliant hand could move,
And rouse its throbbings to a theme of love.
Behold! she waits her patron good and brave,
By the blue waters of Atlantic's wave;
And, cheered by love, long cherished, and last won,
Bathed in a tide whose streams have just begun,
Her notes, aspiring, reach the rounded skies,
And swell in sweetness as their raptures rise.

Hail! Princess, virtuous, world-renowned, beloved!
We bid thee welcome, here so far removed
From Her, whose love has always been thy light;
From that great Queen, who sways a Christian might,
Ruling the movements of one half the world,
With sword unsheathèd, and with flag unfurled.
Oh welcome! is the song of every voice;
Thy welcomes are our nation's chiefest joys.
Though we display no glittering castle-towers,
Nor lovely English vales embalmed by flowers,
Nor bosky parks abounding in choice game,
Nor burnished palaces in golden flame,

Yet, we can give a land that's rich and free,
In Home, in Heart, in Hope, in Liberty,—
An infant empire in the mighty West,
Rocked by three oceans to a native rest;
A virgin soil, a freedom-loving land,
A race that guard it with an iron hand.
We tender thee, a nation's noblest dower,
Brave patriot hearts,—the empire's only power;
And, oh! we pledge by our ancestors' name,
By all that's holy,—by that heavenly flame
That filled the bosoms of the wise and great,
To strengthen monarchy,—protect our State,
To fight for Freedom, and wear Honor's crown,
To strike th' aggressor and the tyrant down,
To rule supreme by valor and by lore,
Or die victorious as our sires before!

Hail! glorious union with our motherland
Hail! Royal pair that strengthens that dear band
Oh, may young Canada's congenial hearth
Protect your virtues, and exalt your worth;
May each broad vale resound with Nature's voice,
To fire the muses of your sacred joys;
May each primeval mount sublimely rise,
And point your spirits to the heavenly prize;
May art's bright flag unfurl on every breeze;
May Science rule our nation still in peace;
May Education stretch her golden wings
And soar to realms whence living wisdom springs;
Till Nature's God commands on Nature's throne,
And skeptic knowledge be for e'er o'erthrown!

MABEL.

(A MEDLEY.)

APOLLO, in his car, descending
  O'er Alleghany's time-worn brow,
Gave one last look and smiled commending,
Upon the green and purple, blending
With golden raptures of his glow;
  The low soft trillings of the birds—
  The thousand-echoed human words
Gave eve their adoration sweet.

A gentle yellow haze now slumbered
  Upon the bosom of the mount;
The troops of sunbeams, red, unnumbered,
Dappled the fleecy sky, encumbered
  With essence from the sparkling fount;
Pervading beauty—loveliness alone
Reclined, in state, upon bright nature's throne,
  Ruling the earth with zephyr wand.

Thus, with glad fascination, swaying,
  Calm twilight held the forest race
Spell-bound; till sombre shades, arraying,
And dallying over rock, and playing,
  And deepening on the valley's face,
Heralded coming eve. Once more
The sun was sinking on the yellow shore,
  And nature languished in a dream.

Pale and mute, was Mabel standing,
  Like some dark statue of old Rome,
Watching below the blue waves stranding
Of the glorious lake that, there expanding,
  Mirrored the evening star's blue home,

With such an excellence of love,
As if the earth were heaven above,
  And God's abode were in the deep.

The river, further on, went moaning
  Its lonely way towards the sea;
While on its banks, sat laughing, groaning,
In jeer, in jest, grimace and yawning,
  Beside their watchfire's blazing glee,
Creatures of wild fantastic form—
Dark spirits like a midnight storm—
  Scions of passion—fiendish sprites.

Tall, swarthy forms, with hawk-eyes peering;
  Grotesquely clad and fearless in fray;
A language, every language nearing;
Mixed manners, to all castes appearing,
  From India to America.
By plunder, thefts, and murder cold,
For lands, for wealth, or tempting gold,
  They did their livelihood maintain.

The honest settler, by oppression
  Compelled to flee his rude chateau,
And to abandon all possession,
Despite appeal or intercession,
  Strength of the sword or courage true,
Fled fast. as doves before a hawk,
O'er mountain-path, a hopeless flock,
  Once more to rear their cherished hope.

Each desperate ruled act and intention;
  Each was his subject and his king;
But *one* alone they dared not mention—
From *her* alone they brooked prevention—
  Her eye alone could rev'rence bring,

One word and that could respect command—
One power subdued—the enchantress wand
  Of Mabel, the Gipsy mother.

Fierce, daring, ruthless, independent;
  With iron will, strong, lightning power,
She had obtained divine ascendant;
Her mind was like a gem resplendent,
  Conspicuous in a ruined tower,
Pregnant still with honest pride,
Though sunk in mis'ry, and denied
  All but the terror of mankind.

Her life was mystery, as her station,
  To all those savage untaught minds;
Nor did they quest her name or nation—
They fancied in imagination
  That she was goddess of the winds—
That, at her magic touch, the earth
Would be dissolved—that time had birth
  Co-eval with her virgin life.

All known was this:—one stormy morning,
  Beneath the refuge of a rock,
Just as the clarion-bird sang warning
Of day, one of the band, returning
  From his depredatory walk,
Espied a woman, bending low,
And singing, softly, words of woe
  Unto two babes of innocence.

Ere long, one child, alone, was kissing
  The bosom of its Gipsy mother;
And, as the autumn winds went hissing,
And, as the winter snow was missing,
  Yet ne'er returned the darling other,

Beneath the cedar of the cave,
The bryony clasps a little grave—
   The grave of the little stranger.

Within that grave, with Essie buried,
   Lay, mouldering, Mabel's hopes and fears;
A something awful, in it, carried
A melancholy, as she tarried,
   Unto her bosom, while she appears
Half-terrified, half-glad, to read
The words she placed at Essie's head,
   With ashen face, and dismal brow :—

THE EPITAPH.

Sleep! gentle Essie, sleep!—
The woodbine is twining
   Over thy grave;
And the wild flowers repining,
   Over thee wave.
   Sleep! Sleep!

Sleep! gentle Essie, sleep!
The leaves they are turning
   Yellow and sear;
Now the mountain is mourning,
   Casting a tear.
   Sleep! Sleep!

Sleep! gentle Essie, sleep!—
The wild wind, careering,
   Passes thee by;
Spring-time is nearing—
   Sadder am I.
   Sleep! Sleep!

Sleep! gentle Essie, sleep!—
The scent-flowers are springing,
Greeting the May;
And the wild warblers singing
Haply of thee.
Sleep! Sleep!

Those simple words of love she hallowed—
A rich, and truthful picture-light
Of those long days of youth, when follow'd
Wisdom, piety, and mirth, now swallow'd
In a sea of misery and night;
And dreaded them, because they stung
Her conscience like a viper's tongue,
With the sharp sense of some black deed

Bright Zoe, a darling gem of nature,
Her mother's joy and sacred care,
In body, mind and beauty, was mature;
A face, like royalty, divinely fair;
Eyes, soft and dreamy, as an eve
In autumn; love that would relieve
The ice from off a poor man's heart.

Pure as the dove, gay as the swallow,
And free as is the mountain air;
Her sweet voice, the soft quivering mallow
Her bosom the zephyr-blown billow;—
The violin, lute and guitar,
Transformed into angels of song,
As swept her fairy hand along,—
Thus fairly accomplished was Zoe.

Led by his youthful fancy's musing,
Forth on the mount did William stray;
Had reached the crest whereon in whiling
The hours to death, she oft sat, smiling

The ruddy flush of life diffusing
His cheek upon; his brow enclosing,
  A thousand auburn ringlets play;
His thoughts forerunning to the spot,
Where fortune cast his natal lot—
  The glorious vale below the cave.

The flowers in varied hues, were flaunting
    Along the labyrinthal path;
The sylvan choir with song enchanting;
The fragrant air was joy implanting;
  And every charm that beauty hath
Too softly soothed his beating breast,
Till sick of joy, he sank to rest
  Within a copse where fragrance bloomed.

DREAM.

The dreamer sees a maiden fair
Stand o'er his bed and shed a tear,
And stooping soft in gentle fear,
  She whispered low and sweetly;
Her brow was alabaster-white;
Her modest cheek was lily-bright;
Her eyes the liquid stars of night;
  Her form attired discreetly.

Anon she wove a blossomed wreath,
From mingling shades of life and death
With honey-lip and balmy breath
  With dew-drops frescoed brightly;
The cresset on his brow she placed,
And rose admiringly in haste,
Then, knelt again, as if misplaced
  She deemed the crown so sightly.

The tedious tide of time beguiling,
  Zoe, filled with strong, unlavished love,

At fair romances, fancy-wove—
By hap, she strayed where William slept;
To flee essayed in vain—she wept—
But tears could not undo the spell.

SONG.

Awake, lovely sleeper!
The day is dead, the west is red,
　The daisy's eye is closing;
Like funeral pall the shadows fall
　Across thy sweet reposing.
Awake! awake! awake!

Awake, lovely sleeper!
The little birds, their vesper words,
　Are mingling sweetly, sadly;
The babbling stream, to kiss the beam
　Of eve, is leaping gladly.
Awake! awake! awake!

Oh wake, lovely sleeper!
For night is drear, and fraught with fear,
　And thou art unprotected;
Oh love, arise, restore my sighs
　The love thou hast exacted!
Awake! awake! awake!

Oh wake, loved one, dear one!
The dewy flower with raptured power
　Around thy brow is wreathing;
Thy bosom tells in gentle swells
　How sweet thy lips are breathing!
Awake! awake! awake!

Oh wake, my love awake!
Thou hast my heart, dare I depart?

I'm bound in iron fetters!
Oh love, awake, and let me take
　From thee Love's mystic letters!
Awake! awake! awake!

　My heart's adored, awake!
To stoop, and sip the honeyed lip,
　Cannot destroy thy pleasure;
The fear thus sweet, I must repeat—
　Now wake, my fount of treasure!
Awake! awake! awake!

With love-dream sigh, young William waking,
　Beheld the kneeling maiden's face
Supremely sweet; his dream forsaking
Left but an ideal sweeter making
　His real life, than all the grace
And transient joy, that prinked the maze,
The moment past, of his sweet dream!

She reeled, and on her pathway, flying
　With fearful step, before his eye,
Wound ledgy path through brushwood swaying—
Breaks her support, she falls, and lying
　In death-like sleep, from dark cliff high
His gaze falls on the maiden lie!
Such mortal joy—such mortal woe—

O'er crag and cleft, he, quick descending,
　Soon kneels the angel fair beside,
And every hopeful art is lending,
To curb the fatal doom impending,
　And to revive the ebbing tide,
Happily life and love allied,
Full soon his noble guerdon proved.

There, as red evening's shadows blended
　With clouds impurpled soft and deep,

The notes of simple love descended
Still down the mount, and, when they ended,
   The quivering tree-leaves seemed asleep,
And every bird did silence keep,
To hear renewed such trusting love.

And oft, when evening's shades were falling
   Across the valley's open breast,
Just as the brow of light was palling,
And warblers, sweet and lonely calling
   Their lovers to the bower of rest,
Trilling with gay romantic zest
Tripped gentle Zoe to William's arms.

Yet, silent, deep in contemplation,
   Half grief, half joy upon her face,
As yielding to a dark temptation,
Or conquered by profound sensation,
   Stood Mabel, the Gipsy grace.
" Zoe lingers on the mountain long,
Her spirit is so leal and strong,"
   Cried Mabel, the Gipsy mother.

While through the rocks these sounds were dying,
   The mountain bosom echoed back
A silvery cadence, soft and sighing,
As an angel's whisper, living, flying
   O'er lake, and brook, and cavern black,
In broken concords mingling sweet;
And as they ceased, to imitate
   The wild bird tuned his quivering lute.

SONG.

I wander on the mountain's brow,
   I wander still forlorn;

No love-light shines upon my path,—
   I weary and I mourn.
Oh, where is he, my soul's lone king,
   My joy, my light, my love!
His eyes were blue—blue like the sea,
   He, gentle as a dove!
Oh, what is life without a love
   To smile the grief away?—
A sullen sky without a sun,
   A night without glad day;
But now, farewell ye hilly scenes,
   The day is waning dim,
I'll hie me to some fair retreat
   To think and dream of him!

Then, as a snow-cloud, light and merry,
   Bathed in the essence of the eve,
With bounding step in graceful hurry,
And features glowing like a cherry,
   She swept towards the Gipsy cave;
And soon she hailed the Gipsy grace,
Who stood in undisguised amaze,—
   With angry scorn her look was fraught.

While, with presumptuous condescension,
   Th'enchantress, towering to full height
Thus spoke :—Sweet Zoe, by what invention'
Or by what spirit's muse—attention!—
   Wert thou inspired? or, on what knight,
Minstrel or bard, or magic power
Didst thou attend, when in the bower
   Thou didst discourse thy love-sick strain?

Daughter, my love is freely given
   To thee, in that thou art alone
The priceless gift I deem from heaven!
My life is thine, my heart is riven
   At any moment for thine own!

One gift, I lavish on thee—love,
'Tis like thyself, breathed from above;
   The only bliss that never rusts!

Daughter, behold yon darkness nearing
   From the far east; so did the night
Press on me with thy life—hearing
I weened, in every breeze, the fearing
   Of death, dishonor, black affright;
Still loved I thee through hard despair,
Till, like a hope-star, from afar
   Thou didst illume my weary life!

And as thy notes this eve descended,
   I hearkened with a love and fear;
I saw, transformed, renewed, amended,
Myself in youth; and when they ended,
   The swelling symphonies sincere
Found echoing-space within my heart,
And sorrow's vail seem'd rent apart,
   And I was young and one with thee.

But when I heard the song of stranger
   Breathe from the bosom of my Zoe,
I thought of some dark mountain-ranger
Who had beguiled thy heart from danger—
   A life brimful of sullen woe—
My tangled life, in faith, returned,
Shrouded in black, cold, sear and burned
   By love's fond passion's boundless sway!

Zoe lowed her head in sorrowing sobbing—
   Long ere her lips could dare reply—
Then told, with aching heart, hot throbbing,
And long-drawn breath her bosom robbing,
   Th' adventure on the mountain high;
Till, as she ceased, eve's twinkling star

Was lost among her sisters fair,
   And sleep reclaimed the silent world.

There are, who, born to state and station,
   Nurtured by pride in room of thought,
Existent still in every nation,
Misname for love hallucination,
   And ignorance for wisdom fraught—
Who seek to circumscribe the way
In which unfettered love should stray,
   Guiding its throbs by science cold.

They are a curse; their laws are erring,
   Reproach to wisdom, open shame;
Their art provokes more dismal fearing,
Dire agony, lust, sin ensnaring,—
   More wreck of life, than sword or flame!
No! fortune cannot give content,
Nor wealth atone for love misspent—
   Love is its only, own reward.

Love is the crystal, life surrounding
   Disposes it to relish joy;
Presents a world with thought abounding;
Protects its craft on shoals from grounding;
   In heart makes human heart rely:—
That spirit pure to mortals given,
When life exulting looks to heaven—
   Love is great life in great devotion.

Oh! happy twain, midst flowers reclining,
   Where that sweet copse its fragrance spreads.
What reck ye of the world's repining,
While love, in joy, its task assigning,
   Showers stars of blessing on your heads?
The arbor leaves their vespers hymn,
The songsters speak their warblings trim,
And life embosoms you as one.

I hear you in that pristine bower ;
    Would to my heart such lot were mine !
Behold you, hallowed by love's power,
    To each, each a protecting tower,
        Arms lock and whispering souls combine !
Oh ! now I see the shallop light
Plunge in the water's bosom bright,
    At distance hear this song :—

BOAT SONG.

THE daylight is ending, the blue waves are stranding,
The stars now are twinkling in peerless delight ;
The woodlands are sighing, our echoes are dying,
The west is still ruddy with perishing light.
Sing, love, oh, sing ! for the pride of the waters—
I'll pull for my blades they are sturdy and true ;
I'll sing for the princess of Beauty's fair daughters,
Rosy her cheek, and her eyes of soft blue.

The pale moon is shining, for lovers divining,
The sky is now crystalline spangled with sheen ;
The boat swiftly moving, we silently loving,
Shall cut through the waves to the river bower green.
Sing, love, oh sing ! though the moments are flying,
Life is not measured by moments of time ;
Sweeter, oh far, is one love-song undying
Than all the fleet seasons that vanish as rime !

May thy dear heart, confiding, unknown to all chiding,
Move peacefully on as the wavelets below—
No storms ever warring, no dark passions marring
The love-light illuming thy bosom's soft flow.
Ripple and sally ye sons of the mountain ;
Sparkle and flash in the moonlight's white glee !
Lovely Diana ! aloft from thy fountain,
Pour down thy sweet rays on my lover and me.

Full through the bower the song is flowing,
　　Each cadence dying softly sweet;
Leal-hearted lovers swiftly rowing
Merrily, merrily, merrily going,
　　The moving oars to music beat;
They kiss the water's quivering lip,
And drink new joys at every dip,
　　Then list the day of lover's lute.

As rich as bright imagination,
　　Reposed the grandeur of the scene;
The banks, embowered in decoration;
Wreath swelled o'er wreath in art's relation,
　　While dancing star-light filled between,
The boughs, festooned from shore to shore,
Left scanty room to ply the oar;
　　The trickling eddies sang beneath.

Adown, the trembling waves dividing,
　　Flew in its pomp the shallop gay
O'er billowy crest in mirth subsiding,
The lovers deemed their joys abiding—
　　Will raptured lovers learn delay?
Turn on your course, ye happy pair!
Reck not to follow joy too far!—
　　In every cup of bliss are dregs.

As springs the wolf on houseless stranger,
　　Or catamount upon its prey,
So, from the bower, the mountain ranger,
His coarse throat filled with sounds of danger,
　　Leaped for the lover's way!
Young William quick discerned their ire,
And bent with more than mortal fire;
　　While Zoe, undaunted, whispered cheer.

C

Stout William's heart was strong and noble
   His brawny arm like iron band;
His common share, he'd met of trouble,
But strength made peril seem a bubble,
   And courage owned his ruling hand,
Against the four, in single might,
He draws his oars with vantage slight,
   And fearless hails his ribald foes;

"Pull, wrangling dogs! I scorn your raving;
   My bride is yours, when ye overtake,
Your sappling muscle aid is craving!
Behold my lover's locks are waving
   Defiant to your anger's ache,
Well for his bride can William die—
Die thrice—but not while oars can play;
   Nor guilt I own, nor insult brook!"

He plied his art in skilful fashion;
   Swift flew the boat along the wave;
His foes had soon subdued their passion,
And homeward turned in contemplation,
   For vandal host love courage brave,
Had not the oar-blade, trebly tried,
Broke at the row-lock by his side!—
   Upon such reeds doth fortune hang.

Within his arms he seized his treasure;
   Plunged fearless in the chilly tide;
Reached for the shore in sturdy measure,—
Forth came the band in mean displeasure,
   And barred him ere he reached the side.
Bravely he fought, but fought in vain
To save his bride from woeful pain—
   He, struggling, fell amid the odds.

A band of Gipsy youth, the rowers,
  Who, envious of fair Zoe's elect,
And actuated by the powers
Of native hate, among the bowers,
  By point agreed, did all collect,
To Mabel's cave they bore him on,
There, chained him to a rock-rent stone
  Unknown to Zoe, who mourned him dead.

By day, by night, alone she wandered,
  Distraction bordering on her mind,
O'er rock and rent where, faint, meandered
Dark, bubbling stream, from cleft engendered
  By secret power; the sorrowing wind
Took up her frantic plaint, and wove
Its echoes through each alpine grove,
  Near to the cave she strayed and sang.

ZOE'S SONG.

No more I hear my William's song,
  No love-notes warm my breast;
Cold are the voices borne along,
  From the far deepening west.
The lay-birds' trill upon the hill,
  All destitute of love,
Floats idly down, from warblers flown
  To join in choral grove.

My day is gone, my night is on;
  Dark sorrow brooding o'er
My lonely soul, the love-lit sun,
  Excludes for ever more!
Oh ye bright skies! could I but rise
  Where your light glory swells—
I, pinioned soft, should mount aloft
  To where my William dwells!

'Tis vainest hope in mortal man
    To seek immortal lore;
Yet Thou above, high Sovereign, can
    Grant wisdom in rich store.
With heavenly fire, my heart inspire
    To anchor faith in heaven;
With seraph star, guide, from afar,
    My soul with sorrow riven.

Gone are the charms that held me true
    To this foul forest life—
Gone is the star that led me through
    The gloomy vale of strife:
Unmingled quiet claims the night;
    The river murmurs low;
Hush! troubled soul, I hear the roll
    Of music soft below!

WILLIAM'S SONG.

Daughter of sorrow! weep not, I pray thee!
    Weep not for bosom as lifeless as mine!
Love more delightful shall heaven repay thee;
    Grief dare not trammel a spirit like thine!

Dark though thy midnight, sunlight is rising;
The clouds are dispersing
    That vail its sweet ray;
Life hath no rapture but sorrow arising
Shall darken its portal
    As evening the day.

Nought, save thy voice
    And the whip-poor-will's warning,
Steals o'er the rocks that encircle my cave;—
Then farewell, my darling!
    I fear not! Ere morning,

These rocks shall entomb me,
  My prison and grave!

Her sorrow-riven bosom trembled;
  The deepest chords of love and woe,
Quick struck as nature's hand preambled,
Gave forth their mingling choirs assembled,
  In notes now high, now low.
She struck, o'er cliff and stone, her course
Where taught, the satyrs warbled hoarse,
  Where demon sprites held nightly court!

Where ledge o'er ledge in bold relieving,
  Sprang from the mountain's mighty chest,
She held her way; her foot receiving,
Each granite table rang deceiving—
  What power can conquer love's warm breast!
Her lover's chains she soon unbound,
And silent, led the pathway round—
  They kissed in joy and parted mute.

A peerless summer eve was waning,—
  The sun had dipped his yellow brow
Into the ruddier liquid, feigning
Repose. The toil-done world complaining
  Of misspent hours and reckless vow.
The cavern door was flung ajar;
Loud grumbled lock and hinge and bar;
  A ruthless form the threshold claimed!

" Be seated, sir! Thy mission broach,
And reason give for thy approach
To this enchanted mountain cell
Which looks to heaven and leads to hell!
If idly, stranger, on thy look
My meaning falls—my hot rebuke
Shall soon efface thy scornful smile
And vaunting gaze, thou scoffer vile!"

" The cause is mine; and moveless still,
I hazard or withhold at will.
I will reveal my purpose here
To *thee* alone, so give me ear."

" Then follow me, and by my faith,
Thou'lt witness soon the shades of death;
For no rash venture, fondly vowed,
Has e'er restored the boaster proud,
Who dares to violate the spell
That haunts each vista of this cell!
Now guard thee well, be liege and true
And follow in thy courage through!

" No sickly child or timid maid,
Who of thy shadows is afraid,
Pursues thy way, but one whose nerve
Has ne'er been taught the sin to swerve;—
To whom Omnipotence has given
No fear of aught beneath the heaven."

She piloted through creviced aisle—
'Mong splintered rocks and fossil pile.
At times the sun's faint darting beam
Came flash across the living dream;
And, as it flickered on the veil,
It seemed a phantom weird and pale,
To which the foot-fall's echoing round
Imparted mortal whispering sound.
At times he scanned the armor dread
Of both the living and the dead;
And grizzly scalps hung on the wall
With hideous heads and courtier's pall.
Then Mabel paused and turned apace,
Triumphant hatred in her face,
And, pregnant with presumptuous fire,
Smiled scorn the stranger to admire!

"Doth fear not vanquish courage now?"
"No, by my soul, no fear I know!"
"Well, dost thou hear the groaning pains
  Of all thy comrades in hot chains—
  Here lie they in their fatal cell
  That soon must be transformed to hell."

Then, to admit light's scanty tide,
She raised the veil of bison's hide;
Whereat a scene of horrid woe
Presented to the ranger's view.
There lay those arms that had maintained
His honor, pulseless, cold and chained.—
There was the form of youth and strength,
Subdued, and shackled low at length;
While imprecation, groan and gyve,
Torment the few who still survive!
But when they spied their chief again,
They each suppressed all sign of pain;
And bore with martyr valor high,
Their sorrows deep with steadfast eye
Unto his band he simply said:—
"Fear not, brave few! raise up the head!'
Whereat each spirit beat anew;
While brow and eye were full aglow.
Such was the reverential power
With which his host owned Merlin Tower.

Then round a lofty spiral stair
Of antique style, she led with care;
Until she touched its summit quite,
Where one lone star held sentry light;
And at its disc she whistled clear;
Responsive sounded clank and jeer,
As if within, a host arrayed
For foe unworthy of their blade,
At one command they issued forth
Like the wild dancers of the north;

On either side the fretted aisle,
They turned in rank from single file;
And stood in quaintest pomp exposed,—
A motley band. Their looks disclosed
A semblance dark of rebel band,
The rude banditti of each land.
They wore skin leggings slashed in silk,
And buckskin sandals white as milk,
And pantaloons of velvet blue,
With fawn-hide vests of mottled hue;
Their eyes were stern, their brows were dark,
Their cheeks tattooed with yellow bark;
They armed with musket, pike and spear,
With mace and lance, and helmet sear.
Here Mabel stood in scorn again,
And tossed her head in haughty pain;
But, seeing that the stranger's eyes
Spoke not of danger or surprise,
She quickly pressed along the pass
And anger's impulse did repress;
Until the way in devious maze,
Enlarged into a vasty space.

" Here, stranger, scorner, scoffer, stay!
Disclose thy mission!—no delay!
If future destiny you seek
Why then so long delay to speak?
To me unmeasured power is given
To look within the pale of heaven;
And rule all things of earth, as well
As burst the iron bars of hell;—
And if thou com'st, intruder bold,
As wolf into a shepherd's fold;
Or seek'st to break the sacred power
That still enchants this fatal bower;
Think not, thou rash imposter, think,
The cup of joy thou'lt ever drink!

For thou shalt wander in disdain
With maddened pulse and crazy brain!"

As in exordium thus she stood,
The ranger scanned in curious mood
The tragic garniture that lined
The limits of the space confined.
Upon the wall's pale face were graved
Dark mythic god, and elf depraved,
And satyrs, sylphs, and monsters grim,
And warriors locked in battle dim.
Upon the cave's granitic floor,
Remotest from the guarded door,
There stood the gray and moisty bone
Of a huge human skeleton.
Whose eyeless caves in horror pore,
Inanimate for ever more:
Around each limb, in shiny fold,
A serpent wound in deadly hold,
Resting his head upon the breast
Where life had long since sunk at rest.
His eyeballs flashed envenomed fire,
Dull rattles spoke his nimeous ire.

This vicious grandeur came to sight
By a sweet star whose filmy light,
In pearly beams poured softly down—
The sweet coronal of a crown,
Throned in the ceiling's stony brow,
And but revealed in twilight glow;
For all was purposed to inspire
The rash intruder with a fire
That would devour all human pride,
And drown its flames in fear's strong tide.

But courage more than mortal dower
Lived in the ranger Merlin Tower,

He viewed each scene without concern,
And curled his lip in open scorn,—
Enraged by such effectless course,
He rose in vocal accents hoarse.

" Think'st thou, false sorceress, to appal
My spirit with this graven wall,
Or with the bones of this dry frame,
' Or with this serpent's eye of flame ?—
Think'st thou the groans of yon dark cell
Can my intrepid soul repel ?
Ha ! no, each but rekindles strife ;
Each fills anew the streams of life !
Time passes like yon bubbling stream—
We see it rippling in the beam ;
But as its waters hurry by,
They fade forever to the eye ;
Nor may we guess what freight may bear
Adown the tide ; we only dare
Behold the fleet when sweeping past,
With swelling sail and giddy mast.
The present lot is ours alone ;
It is our all—the past is gone ;
The future never was, nor is,
Nor ever will be ; it is His
Who, veiled in mystic light, conceals
His greater power, and but reveals
Light adequate unto our need ;
Not our desire demands His meed.
My purpose ?   It is wise and brief ;
You are a queen, I am a chief—
You know our warring clans have shed
Their blood like water, and the dead
Lie slumbering upon vale and hill,
Their dust proclaiming vengeance still.
Hear ! should this warfare be prolonged,
Can slaughter gratify the wrong'd ?

You have a child, a daughter rare
In beauty, and of promise fair;
I have a son, bold, young and firm,—
True is his brawn, his bosom warm;
Now as commissioners of war,
Let us depute this well-matched pair;
While we will pray to heaven above
That war's red hands may clasp in love;
That strength united own our band
And freedom bless our bosky land!"

" Agreed! to-morrow at the dawn
Seek thou again our lintel-stone;
Bring with thy son, ten warriors bold,
The bravest watchers of thy fold:—
If such be the decrees of fate,
These shall the nuptials celebrate;
If not I'll marshal ten of ours,
We'll let them close among the bowers,
Until there stands a single man
To lift the blade for chief or clan;
When we shall tie the bonds of peace
And yield our passions to their ease.
But he, who conquers for his chief,
Shall claim the dual realms his fief.
But stay, thou art so true and bold;
I would to thee a theme unfold—
A theme that haunts my deepest soul
With nightly fears; whose shadows roll
Around my every moment's path
Like spirits from the realms of wrath!
'Tis of my life; but thou must say
Thou'lt ne'er disclose it, till the day
I close my eyes in sleep of death;—
It comes ere long; this hoary wreath
Foretells it near—oh, may it come
And take me to a happier home!

Oh, green were the vales of old England,
   Sweet, sweet was the silvery morn;
Oh, cheery the English castle-home,
   On the day that my being was born!

Oh, glad were the eyes of my parents,
   As they gazed on their legacy bright,
Deeming little that blossom so blessed
   Should ripen to fruit of the night!

Oh, white were the sands of the sea-shore,
   When first on their beauty I gazed,
As the blue waves 'low dancing and laughing,
   My soul with their splendor amazed!

That day was the happiest, and holiest,
   Ever dawned on the paths of my life;
When both father and mother caressed me,
   With the rapture of husband and wife.

How I see them arise through the vistas
   Of years in their hurry flown by—
How the past seems to come like a phantom,
   Then dissolve like a mist to the eye.

My sire was a duke of old England,
   Hot with chivalrous blood of the knight—
High, dark, foreign brow, sable waved locks—
   Tall, slender, with eyes sloe and bright.

My mother—immaculate lily—
   With Saxon blue eyes like a dove,
Was happy, congenial, and modest,
   A queen from the dreamland of love!

Thus I passed the sweet days of my childhood,
   In alternative shelter and shade;

When stormy, I ran to my father,
   When mild, with my dear mother play'd.

But the spirit of fancy and fiction,
   That coursed through the veins of my sire,
Rose higher and higher within me,
   And filled me with passionate fire!

Oh, the red sun of autumn was blazing,
   And the clouds were like rubies on high,
And the laurel leaves rustled in whispers,
   To the dalliant wind with a sigh,

When we parted with garden and castle,
   And the minaret glittering soft—
Left the chapel and pastor beloved,
   Left the coppice on mountain aloft.

The blue waves, those children of ocean,
   Beat athwart the white beach and recoiled,
While the vessel was rocking impatient
   For the throng that so busily toiled.

To Italia's clear, genial climate,
   We pressed with unmingled delight,
Past green, sunny islands of spices,
   Successively waning from sight.

Ah! well I remember the glory
   That pensively breathed on each scene—
The statuesque piles of the city,
   The odorate valleys so green.

Ah! well, too, yet I remember
   The soft, lucid liquid of lakes,
Embosomed in valleys ambrosial—
   Sad memory! how my heart aches.

The mulberry, fig tree, and olive
  There bloomed in their turn side by side;
The sugar-tree, orange, palmetto,
  Hung their luscious fruit o'er the tide.

Then forth came Italia's daughters,
  In silk and in blossoms arrayed;
And they sang 'neath the pure sky of Parma,
  Till the evening star lit the shade.

But the joys of this life are but transient!
  Fleet, fleet as the shadows of pride—
That mother, my mother, my treasure,
  Was beckoned across the dark tide!

Our tears we migled in sorrow,
  As lonely we journeyed below;
And the happiest pageant of gladness
  But deepened our potions of woe.

But my father soon changed his demeanor,
  All his heart seemed alight and aflame;
Yes! a beauteous princess of Florence
  Soon bowed to my lost mother's name!

Her dusky brown visage I pondered,
  Her arrogant mien and array;
She glittered in garnet and sapphire,
  But she cherished no love toward me.

I fled in my anguish and frenzy—
  I fled, how I know not, nor where;
I wandered alone through the vineyards,
  In grief and unuttered despair.

Till I found a home and a refuge,
  In a hut on the "Appenine Height"

Indwelt by a frail old magician,
  "The spirit of the dark and the light."

It stood by a gorge in the mountain,
  On the mule-path from Venice to Rome;
And many a pilgrim, at eve-tide,
  Would find in our hovel a home.

Strange stories they'd tell of the city,
  Of Venice, the town on the wave,
Of the galley and swart gondolier,
  Of Doge, and podesta, and slave.

And they carried to Rome to the Pontiff
  Their plumes and their tassels and curls.
Their diamonds, their perfumes and coral,
  Their amethysts, opals, and pearls.

To purchase remission from evils,
  To have their souls washed and made pure,
To redeem their beloved ones from purg'try,
  To make passage to heaven secure;

And each pilgrim, crossing his person,
  And counting his rosary prayer,
Bow'd thrice at the door of our hovel,
  Praying the enchantress appear.

Questing his fate in the crevasse,
  Through which he must journey disguised,
In the garb of an artist or friar,
  To conceal what the banditti prized.

She would prophesy fame or misfortune,
  Beseeching in sorrow or joy
To beware of the tribes of the valley,
  Who pilgrims sought to destroy.

Then, turning his vesture of damask
    From its spangled and glittering fold,
He'd pour out rich presents of coral,
    Perfumed with rare ottar, and gold.

Returning, if fortune so favored,
    He charmed us with Florence and Rome;
How they shone in their orient grandeur,
    Illumined by temple and dome.

Such a life and vocation entranced me,
    More happy I grew day by day;
For I loved the romantic and mystic,
    And the splendor of foreign display.

There, I saw how the sorceress conquered
    By the force of her character sear—
There I learned that fatality's being
    Had source in humanity's fear.

When the cold hand of death struck her vitals,
    And the hour of departure drew nigh,
Then I sank her to rest in the valley,
    As the silvery orbs lit the sky.

Once more on the wide world of sorrow—
    Once more on the ocean of wrath—
Once more, lonely, frantic, and friendless,
    I strayed on my desolate path.

Till I joined a host of banditti,
    Infesting crevasse and ravine;
Their life of romance and aggression
    Well suited my passionate mien.

The adventurous student and poet
    All flocked with an ardent desire

To our camp, for our legends and customs
   Set their bosoms impulsive afire.

In the medley, came a young songster,
   Of princely and elegant mould;
His name was embellished with titles,
   And his vestures embroidered in gold.

Then he sang me fond songs of my beauty,
   And told me such tales of his love,
That I sacrificed all to his honor—
   Turned gentle and mild as a dove.

I loved him beyond all conception,
   With a first, that most heavenly zeal;
Yes, though he has caused me my ruin,
   My love for him still I can feel!

It was spring, and the mountains and valleys
   Grew instinct with symbols of life,
When hands, hearts, and loves were united—
   He kissed me, and called me his wife.

Then back to the city he wended,
   For our love to prepare a sweet home;
And many a vesper song warbled,
   Went following where he did roam.

One morn, as the gray mists ascending
   Forsook the green valley's soft breast,
That beauteous virgin, an infant,
   Was laid on my bosom at rest.

I thought not of good, nor of evil,
   Nor of shame, nor reproach, nor of pain;
I beheld but the glorious image
   Of him whom I sought to regain.

Soon I took the fair thing in my arms,
   Heart-rended, weak, weary, and sore;
I journeyed, persistently journeyed,
   Till I stood at my image's door.

The tranquil of evening had settled;
   Soft voices, low, merry, and sweet,
Fell hot on my curious conscience—
   My heart not enduring to beat.

I peered through the window's bright lattice,
   Great God! I went mad! I espied
A gorgeous bride with a beautiful babe—
   And my husband sat whispering beside!

The truth of my shame beamed around me,
   Like a star at the dawning of day,
I beheld my young virtue in ashes—
   My life and my love, led astray!

I crept to their couch as they slumbered—
   I pierced his fair bride to the heart;
I flew with the wings of distraction—
   But where, I knew not—like a dart!

When again to my conscious spirit
   The language of reason returned,
I stood on America's mountains,
   With memory saddened and burned.

I knew not what magic or power
   Bore me over Atlantic's broad brine;
But I know in my frantic confusion
   I seized both *her* infant and mine!

I cared for the gentle young sisters
   With affection and motherly love,

But Essie, the cheerless young orphan,
   Soon passed to a mother above.

Here I've practised the art of enchanting
   And soothsaying, nurtured in youth,
For none ever knew on this mountain
   Of my history or lineage, truth.

While voiceless grief her looks disclosed,
With trembling step and mien composed,
She led the stranger to the light
Then sank insensible in night;
Till woe, from its obscuring clouds,
Poured out its scalding, hurrying crowds,
And all the soul-dregs of the past
Had swept away before its blast.
Happy, repentant in sweet pain
Her youthful self she rose again.
The clouds had rolled themselves away—
Her starry night was almost day—
The past, a blank; the future, bright—
Bright with the new-begotten light!
With every feature soft and mild
She sought her beauteous, artless child
Whom, glowing in her twilight bliss
She greeted with a holy kiss.

"Daughter, take cheer! the morn is dawning,
   War's night is o'er, and blessed peace
Restored! This demon, grovelling, fawning
   Is at an end. Hope's joy, atoning,
      Yields to thy faith a sweet increase!
At last, yon golden star aloft
Pours down its breathing effluence soft!
   Daughter, take cheer, the morning dawns!"

"Oh mother! what strange star is burning
   Upon thy brow—upon thy cheek?

BOYHOOD HOURS.

Thy hope doth wear the robes of mourning!
Tell me, dear mother! on returning—
  For lo, thy eyes do volumes speak—
From parley with that fearful chief,
What theme has given thee relief
  Why speak of Faith, Light, Hope and Peace?"

" Hear then, sweet angel, our peace-off'ring!
  The chieftain's son is fair and free!
To end all warring, vengeance, suffering,
This is the term of mutual proffering:—
  The chieftain's son shall wed with thee,
And this foul war which thou dost hate
We shall in happy peace abate;
  And after, own us thine and thine!"

" Oh, mother, dearest! hear me praying!
  I cannot, must not, wed this man;
For, in my heart, a hero staying
Holds it eternal, unbetraying!
  Dear mother, break! oh, break! thy plan—
The man I love is William Tower,
My heart, my soul, myself, my power,
  Whom I released from bondage dire!"

" Daughter, thou lovest me; and loving
  Me, in obedience must await.
Lo! what a piteous carnage, moving,
Have caused these wars! and though reproving
  Every decree I caught from fate,
Thou, now, dost hold thyself in pride,
From truceful means by fate supplied!
  Close rended cloud! we rather night!"

"I love thee mother! In demonstration,
  Black let him be, churlish, self-seeking,
Wed him I shall, in ostentation,
Of all I have, give him oblation,

MABEL.

A thousand hearts, but have not one.
Mother, I'll wed the chieftain's son,
To prove I love thee, war detest!

The morning sun broke through the cloud,
The warblers whistled sweet and loud,
As, down the mount, the sturdy band
Pass careless, till at peace they stand,
By mandate of their leader brave,
Moveless athwart the Gipsy cave.
At Mabel's hest, her stern decade
Soon lined afront with shield and blade.
Fearless, they halted face to face,
With weapons drawn and eyes ablaze,
Awaiting thus the fatal word
For each to quench his thirsty sword.
While thus in desperate poise they stood,
In richest garb, and gayest mood,
Mabel, in right, majestic mien,
Took William's arm, and passed between;
From host to host cheer vied with cheer,
That died in sylvan echoes clear.
With love and hope the hero's breast,
To meet his bride, was fraught and blest.
Full well assured, and joy'ed to meet
The life that made his life so sweet;
But all his hopes were soon o'ercast,
Ere scarce the lintel post he passed,
For lo! reclining on her couch,
He view'd his bride, nor word nor vouch
Availed to rouse her fearful mind,
From dull despair in which she pined.
Her heart, at every sobbing strain,
Seemed rent asunder with the pain;
The votive youth could brook no more,
But crossed in haste the cavern floor,
And, now, oblivious to each rule
Designed by science, art or school

BOYHOOD HOURS.

At nature's universal word,
Embraced his own—his mountain-bird;
And as he kissed her beauteous brow
He whispered sweetly, sweetly, "Zoe!"
The voice had power; it thrilled her through;
Enshrined her in a hope anew,
She hazarded to ope her eyes;
A moment smiled in joy's surprise;
Then, clasped him in admiring love
His heart's bright queen, his turtle dove!

Young William led her from the cave,
Where stood the soldiers rude and brave,
Who, as they viewed her silken gown
Of white, her gemmed and sparkling crown
With amaranthine tissue wrought,
A trousseau rich, as e'er was sought;
And viewed her clinging to the arm
Of William Tower's gallant form,
Divining well the glad affair,
Cleft, with their cheers, the mountain air;
Each seized his foeman by the hand,
Calling him soldier brave, and friend.
Thus joy was crowned, and conflict hushed,
Peace was exalted, warfare crushed,
The chains unbound, the captives freed,
The lovers wed by fate decreed.

SPES GLORIÆ.

Ah me! how lonely, lonely, are the hours
This night. Cold solitude has caught me in
Its greedy arms, and age alone disputes,
With savage frown, her rude demand. Oh yes,
I'm tired of this world! Voices whisper—
I look around, again to see some face
Sweetly familiar to my sight, but find,
The sound comes from my peopled soul, where dwells,
In deep recess, eternally enshrined,
A word or laugh that slumbers there obscure,
Till waked by recollective Sorrow's touch.
O merry laugh, haunt me no more! I'm old
And lonely. On my brow, no sunny smile
To catch thee in the echo! seek some heart
Youthful, and leal and happy—gambol *there*,
Oh child, I feel thee playing with my hair!
I clasp thy hand; what none! oh mind! are these
All thy imaginings? Or sometimes is
There such a narrow bridge between the worlds,
That hands can reach across and smiles be seen
And voices startle? No! no! these are but
The sombre shadows, and the breeze, that find
Their motion in a lonely swaying tree,
No sound! Dull silence! fear doth love thee much!
The fire, like me, grown quite contemplative,
Scarce sends his drowsy glow to cheer the hour,—
Yet, we alone, survive the room within—
Live but are slowly, surely dying.
His glow, like mine, is paled and both shall soon
Sleep in their silent ashes! Speak fire, for
Thy sullen word to me is hallowed! Thy smoke,
My spirit, ascending, leave us both; ah yes!
Thy smouldering flame becomes the record of
My life. Fancy takes form and language there,

Forms come and go, and in their giddy mirth
Before me dance, smiling in youth!

         Come back,
Oh happy days! Youth rosy, sweet, and free,
Return! Come back ye joyous, joyous, hours
When love's warm flame first filled my boyish heart
With eloquence, and gave my spirit's ear
To know the numbers of the stream and rose!
Come back my friends! Why have *ye* left me thus?
Did not I love thee dearer than myself?
Why have all those who strengthened me in strength
In weakness left my side? They sleep! My wife—
My children—ah the sting!—all gone!—all gone!
How much I've seen, and loved, and suffered! Alas!
Rest, rest, ye fairest of the earth; and know
That if the lonely husband, sire and friend,
Who lingers here, would think a wish of thee,
It is that ye are all his loved in happiness!

The fire has died; the light become extinct;
In darkness, death and silence brood. I hear
No mocking laugh; I see no faces fair;
Nor do my hoary hairs wander as in touch!
But through the tears that tremble on my eyes,
I view, from out the darkness here, a smile—
The light of laughter breaking through the night!
And, guided by its radiant power, I see
Distant, approaching the marvellous realms
Of the unseen! I upward fly, and o'er
The intervening mountain, throned in clouds,
A crystal sea looms faintly, yet expands
In glorious roll before my gaze! Hearken!
Oh soul! What is't thou hearest? Rising soft,
Like sweetest music, mingling with the breeze
Of morn, and louder, louder, sweeter yet
It grows! I cannot find its source! Nor can

I see its author, for around, each star
And creature joins in the refrain divine!
Ten thousand, thousand notes exultant rise
From out yon joyous host. They beckon me!—
I follow raptured. Where am I? Who are
These soft winged doves that hover o'er my brow?
This golden gate, how beautiful! Where leads?—
It opens! My friends of youth—of age—my wife—
My children glorified, we meet again!
O throne of love! *My Saviour!*—Thine!—Amen!

LONG AGO.

THERE is a grandeur on the shore
Where twilight lingering dwells,
Where Æolus is sighing love,
In music that excels;
But grander than the rolling flood,
Or the zephyr's softest flow,
Are the glad, old scenes of youth and love,
The scenes,—the scenes of long ago.

We love the friends that are true to us,
The friends who can smile or sigh,
As the star of life is bright aloft
Or sinks till its light must die,
We love the heart that beats with ours,
The hand that can help in woe;
But we'll not forget those dearest friends,
The friends,—the friends of long ago.

In rosy bower, in evening hour,
When pearly dew-drops fall,
Sweet are the song of the maids we love,
Or muse in the festal hall;

But from the tomb of the dead old past,
Illumined with memory's glow,
Spring up the songs of departed lips,
The songs,—the songs of long ago.

The world seems bright with splendor's glow
Where once no glory smiled;
The voice of ease is singing now
Where the hand of labor toiled;
But though we bless the laugh for the sigh
And the joy for the weary woe
Can we forget those days? Ah no,
The days—the days of long ago.

LOVE'S GLORIFICATION.

(Dedicated to M——.)

Raptured soul, oh, call thy numbers
From the chaos of repose;—
Invoke conceptive Fancy from her shade!
Touch thy languid chords, till symphony
My bosom overflows
With warm love-diffused effulgence undelayed

In the darkness, in the deadness,
In the hermitage of thought,
Prometheus-like, oh heart, hast thou been chained!
Now, recall thy warbling turtles
To their long-forsaken cot;
Bid them chant the vestal freedom love-regained.

For the adamantine bondage,
Light-precluding colonnades,
That stood, like giant tyrants, round thy throne,

LOVE'S GLORIFICATION.

Have dissolved in airy shadows
At Love's mystical chamades !—
Life's light and laughter peerlessly atone.

Night no longer plumes her pinions
Perched in portals of my heart,
Nor regnant brood the scions of Despair ;
For through the rosy avenues
That wander to Life's mart
Comes Morn's ethereal effluence bursting fair !

And the sleepy tides whose billows,
Chid by Melancholy's wand,
Beat slow and low in deathlessness of death,
Now in limpid splendor leaping,
Kiss the efflorescent strand,
Bearing strange supernal fragrance in their breath.

All the withered flowers of Fancy,
All the broken notes of song,
Unnurtured by the dew, or heart-forgot,
In faithful amaranthine, now
Reglow in primal throng,—
Renew voluptuous descants heaven-taught.

'Tis a maiden's throbbing bosom,
Filled with sanctifying love,
That wakes in me this aftermath of Faith ;
For I drink reviving essence,
From the golden vase above,
That gives me day in night, and life in death !

From the soul-revealing twinkles
Of her love-inspiring eyes,
Mellow, palpitating fluid radiates,—
Breaking through my prison darkness,
As a ray from paradise,—
Throwing open heaven's gold and jasper gates.

On Existence' sable banner,
She has traced Life's true design,
Enshrined in pinken passion flowers of youth—
The royal red camelia,
And the purple Columbine,
With white lilies twining round the motto "Truth."

Not mean lispings of vain mortals,
Not imagination's art,
Not the eloquence begemmed with poet's light
Can daguerrotype the majesty
Enthroned within her heart,
Or make the canvas glow so matchless bright.

Resplendent, as the glory
Of undying, amber morn,
Heart-adored, the beacon vigils me from strife;
Not in transitory flickers,
But in tranquil constancy,—
The hallowed apotheosis of life.

Quaintly magic interminglings
Of ineffable delight
Linger laughing, round the crimson, dewy lip;
While on the classic perfectness
Of cheeks supremely bright,
Is a dimple where the gods are wont to sip!

Raptured heart! oh, call thy numbers
From the chaos of repose!
Invoke the pensive muses from their shade!
Strike the languid chords, till symphony
My bosom overflows,
And expiring echoes reach the heavenly maid.

THE CHILDREN.

What time I walk my daily path,
The little children round me play;
I see them dancing on the heath;
I hear them laugh the hours away.

Like stars, their eyes are sparkling bright;
Their voices rippling like the stream;
Their feet as ruddy, hearts as light,
As rosy morn's first dancing beam.

And while they sing the chorus loud,
Their youthful bosoms throbbing high,
They seem with voices sweet endowed,
As warbling children of the sky!

Within their minds there is no space
For distant, cold, unborn to-morrow;
No sullen cloud obscures the face
Of their pure sky, with pain or sorrow.

New fancies rise at every breath,
Fresh charms at every step appear;
While hope smiles to the gates of death
And Faith forbids the faltering tear.

For them, the song of every breeze
Is sweetened by the blooming sod;
To them, the music of the trees,
Is nature speaking to her God.

'Tis theirs to pluck the flaunting flowers,
That hang like drooping orbs of gold;
'Tis theirs to ramble through the bowers
And sing the songs we loved of old.

Theirs are the broad and verdant field,
The stream, the forest, and the fountain;
Theirs are the shades the valleys yield,
The lofty kingdom of the mountain!

All theirs the glory of the morn,
The fulgent excellence of day;
All theirs is Luna's silvery horn,
The glittering host in night's array.

Throughout this world, this strange, old world,
I meet them sporting everywhere,
When leaves of spring are yet unfurled,
Or when the autumn woods are bare.

As flowers that grow in desert spots,
To cheer the lonely pilgrim on,
They twine about our words and thoughts,
Inspiring hope when hope is gone.

Oh, happy, happy, youthful hearts!
Oh bounding spirits young and glad!
How little do you feel the darts
That pierce man's soul and drive him mad!

How lightly do you bear the load,
The curse, the darkness, and the toil;
How sprightly do you trip the road,
Nor sink beneath its lustred foil!

Your sorrows are but flakes of snow,
That melt, aud moisten in your mirth;
In grief, your tears can overflow
And drown the tyrant in his birth!

You know not of the darkened soul,
The toiling brain that will not rest,

The awful floods that ever roll,
Within the bondage of the breast !

You know not of the stfled sighs,
The swelling sobs that never burst,
The long-loved hope that silent dies,
Nor thinks to force its fetters curst !

You know not of the feeble knee,
The faltering hand, the palsied arm,
The sunken eyes that dimly see,
The pallid cheek without a charm !

You know not of the breaking heart,
The noisless, toilsome, gnawing pain,
The burning tear, that will not start,
The past, that will not live again !

The sorest pains on all this earth,
Those who endure can only know ;
We all are martyrs to our worth,
We wear the cross the crown forego !

But, long as on the grassy plain,
We see the sportive children play,
We'll dream *us* children o'er again,
And smile *our* phantom fears away.

LOVE'S LEGEND.

WEIRD and wild, on the fleet south wind,
    The rural song is going ;
Across my path, with fragrant breath
    The voice of Spring is flowing ;

The western sky in vernal joy
   With patines gold is burnished;
The feathered crowd are trilling loud
   Their songs with swift wings furnished.

Come, darling, come, and let us seek,
   Where sombre shades are deeping,
A mossy nook by the rippling brook
   In which the flowers lie sleeping.
As the dewdrops sleep on thy rosy lip,
   The breeze with thy tresses playing,
I'll drink new joys, from thy soft blue eyes,
   The smile on thy cheek delaying.

We'll whisper low of the dreams of youth,
   How days, like dreams went fleeting;
The stars as they rise in the azure skies
   Shall vigil love's mystical meeting;
While the moon on her march 'neath the spangled arch,
   A sea of cloudless glory,
From her sceptred clime, shall smile sublime,
   Like the charm of an ancient story.

When the world's rude voice shall be chained at rest,
   The world's cold eye aclosing,
I'll tell thee, love, of a gentle dove,
   Who is now in her grave reposing.
Her eyes were blue. of the Saxon hue
   A star in each was shining
Her cheeks aglow, her brows as snow,
   Like yon moon in the vault reclining

As a silken veil, down her classic brow,
   The sable threads hung loosely;
O'er her bosom rare, on her cheeks so fair,
   They clustered most profusely;

She was sweet in mien, as a heav'n-born queen—
  She was a fairy creature,—
Immortal love in her bosom wove
  And hallowed every feature

We had tripp'd along, with a gladsome song
  To the old log school with pleasure;
We had both been born on a bright June morn,
  Our joys were a common measure;
We grew at length, to prime and strength,
  We grew in fond affection,
As each fleeting day revolved away,
  Our hopes approached perfection.

Splendidly bright, as the evening star,
  In its crystal couch reposing,
Was the light she cast on my soul oppressed,
  When the gates of Hope were closing;
When the world's vain toil, man's angry broil
  Would darken life's radiant portal;
Then her peerless blue eyes were my mirror of joys,
  There dwelt my rapture immortal.

Roaming alone through the woody dell,
  The mingling cowbells chiming,
With a far ding dong, all the green hills among
  Or mead with its river rhyming;
In Fancy's dream, with a gladdening gleam,
  She would rise to the mind's conception,
And I paused to sigh with a love-moist eye
  Till the spell would find adoption.

Both day and night, as a guardian light,
  The mystical lamp was burning,
Illuming my path, from the wiles of wrath,
  My heart from the sea of mourning;

But the flame of faith was quenched by death,
   By the fang of fate love perished,
As an Autumn day, she faded away,
   A dream or a flower fond cherished.

While she moved in the world of time,
   Her love-lit eye still shining,
'Twas my only pride, to call her my bride
   And banish all repining;
And, when she fled with the voiceless dead,
   My every thought was sorrow,
And my soul would burst, from its fetters curst,
   As I dreamed of the gloomy morrow.

Now dry all the tears from thy tender cheek,
   My legend of sorrow is ended;
Full well do I know of the doubts and throe
   In thy young heart's shrine have blended;
To my darling two, I shall still be true,
   Since this sweet hope is given;
Your matchless worth, I may love on earth,
   Yet love my lost in heaven!

THE SAILOR'S PRAYER.

I.

God of the mighty deep!
   Whose awful roar
Breaks our still vigil's sleep!
   We're far from friend or shore!
Loud thunder swells in every treacherous wave,—
Death hisses from the cresting foam—O save
Thy sons of ocean! O God, above the rave

And fury of the storm,
   Hear Thou the sailor's prayer!
Stretch forth thy mighty arm!
Though land be distant, Thou art near!

II.

God of unmeasured strength!
   Those mountains dark
That heave their curling length—
   These are Thy work.
From sleep profound within the glassy brine
They burst in anger at a word of Thine
And close in horrid strife! O Thou divine
   Omniscient Captain! Speak
As of old, on Galilee,
   Father of Might! Oh, break
The power of death lashing the sea!

III.

Father of mercy, pity, love,
   The widows' God!
Between thy cherubim, oh, move!
   Stretch forth thy rod
Of glory, majesty and might! The wail
Of anguish—stifling throbs of prayer,
Wrung from the souls we love, afar, oh, hear!
Our sweethearts, wives and children! Accents frail
   From their sweet lips of innocence and love,
Will surely wing above the deafening gale
   To Thy bright throne above
Oh hear Most High!—
Beside our cabins, door,
On yon far distant shore,
Where the billows hoarsely snore,

Stand our wives convulsed, pale,
In the withering, weltering gale,
Their hearts are rent, distressed,—
A babe on every breast.
O'er the wide and watery main,
Bring us home to them again!
God of heaven hear their prayer:—
" Bring them home to us again, God of the storm!
" Bring our husbands home again, God of love!
" If they sink into the deep, into everlasting sleep,
" When their brave hearts cease to beat
" With the sailor's dauntless heat,
" May their spirits, Father, rise
" To Thy kingdom in the skies
" Dead or living be their God,
" O our Father!"

Brave boys, struggle through the blast;
Should we conquer it at last,
God be praised!
We have prayed, let us toil,
With hope our bosoms warm,
We will grapple with the storm,
Ho! ho! boys, ho! ho! pull away!
If we're conquered by the blast,
We will perish on the mast,
God shall dry the widow's tears,
He shall soothe the orphans' fears.
God be praised! God be praised, Amen!

PRIDE.

'Twas a meaningless, harmless word,
  Spoken to test love's truth,
But it pierced like a poisoned sword
  The hope and the heart of youth;

For it grew and revelled and sighed
At the feasts of the demon Pride.

The light of their love delayed,
   Perished the joy of the past,
And the spirit of faith decayed,
   Till it faltered in death at last;
For anger arose from the tide
That flowed from the fount of Pride.

Their lives have no sacred charm,
   Their eyes no language of mirth,
Their souls are involved in storm,
   In the winds of the bitter north;
For pride and anger and care
Have nurtured and bred despair.

The golden tinted morn,
   With dew-incensed brow,
Bursting on earth forlorn,
   With heavenly light aglow,
Can wake not a slumbering power,
For love hath forsaken her bower.

The blushing and dappling eve,
   The sun on his rubied throne,
The choral band—the sunlit wave,
   Or the day of labor done,
Can never restore that warmly throb
That th'envious hand of pride did rob.

Oh Love! thou prettiest flower,
   The only blessing given
To guide us in the evil hour,
   And pilot our path to heaven;
Yet still, in the sinful passions' train
There is not a brier but may give thee pain.

TO ONE I LOVE.

Were all the sky one blue expanded scroll;
   The sun a quenchless fount of golden ink;
My alphabet, the stars that nightly roll
   Their pearly orbits round the azure brink;
My vigil-lamp, yon phosphorescent moon;
   My pen, a sunbeam; my compositors,
The angels pouring from celestial throne,
   With lightning press, my heart's sweet characters;
A volume I'd compile as great as heav'n,
   And have it cinctured with a zone of pearl,
The key interpretative to thee given,
   That its mysteriousness thou might'st unfurl—
One deep, eternal song inscribed to thee
   And all its gist *my love, my love* to Thee!

THE SUMMER SABBATH MORN.

The voice of labor's wheel is hushed, no sound falls on the ear,
Save the voluptuous matin-note of warblers singing clear;
The universal Sabbath rest of Nature and of God
Hath breathed its sweet quietus and sacred joy abroad.
From the far east, the rubied cloud has sailed, on wings, away;
And the raptured bosom of the sky proclaims the birth of day.
Up from his burnished chariot-couch, imperial Phœbus hies,
To dry with sympathetic smile the tear from nature's eyes;
While sable Erebus forsakes the region of the blest,
And wraps his dark funereal veil on the portals of the west.

THE SUMMER SABBATH MORN.

Oh! Morn most hallowed! Sabbath morn, upon whose angel smile,
Looms not a cloud of guilt or woe, breathes not the sound of toil;
There is a grandeur in thy life, a magic loftier far
Than all the glittering pomp of wealth, the pageantry of war;
There is an eloquence of love, in thy soft arched brow,
That not the fairest touch of Art or Science can bestow;
There is a splendor glorified by thy deep reign of peace,
When power and wealth are slumbering, and human passions cease,
When the frivolity and pride of human lust repose,
When Nature praises Nature's God, and Hope's bright river flows.
Methinks upon Creation's morn, when, new-born in the arch,
The myriad constellations bright, assumed their silent march;
Such peerless joy ineffable had dawned on mortal eyes,
Such radiance must have filled the earth, and reigned in paradise!
Methinks, that, when the warning bell shall toll its last deep knell,
And all the ransomed host arise 'mid glories that excel,
Transcendant beauty, such as this, shall animate, amaze,
And cause each swelling heart to rise in everlasting praise!

And now, with holy, happy hearts, the family choir is singing,
And now, with sacred, solemn peal, the Sabbath bells are ringing,
In swells of softest symphonies, they fill the morning air,
And call the weary sons of toil to the synagogues of prayer.
Adown the long, still avenues, of cool sequestering trees.
The temple sends her sweet appeal on morning's murmuring breeze;

And out among the rural hills, and cheerful country
    domes
It breaks to still the struggling souls and solemnize their
    homes,
"Forth from the haunts of sin and woe, come forth ye
    sons of sorrow,
Nor let salvation, free to-day, be death, remorse to-
    morrow,
Come forth, ye weary sons of toil, released from labor's
    wheel!
Accept the precious rest and peace the gospel truths re-
    veal!
Come forth ye thirsty, hungry, sad, to where abundance
    dwells,
To that eternal fount of love, from which salvation wells!
Come forth, all ye, whose noble parts are canopied in
    night
And bask in the Sabbatic bliss of heaven's effulgent light!"

OR EVER.

Or ever the vestal star of eve
    Shall have couched in the pearly west,
Or ever the gloomy veil of night
    Shall have sunk on the world at rest,
My lover shall know that I love him,
    That a maiden's heart *can* be true,
That I only concealed expressing
    My love till it stronger grew.

Or ever the rays of beauteous morn
    Shall have shed on the love-lorn earth,
Or ever the huntsman's silvery horn
    Shall have spoke its matins forth;

My lover shall troth a token,
  To me of his love so sweet;
Or the spell of my life be broken,
  And this bosom shall cease to beat!

Or ever I break my vows, love,
  Those vows of life and death,
Or ever *thou* break thine own, love,
  This heart shall still in death!
My smiles thou once did prize, love,
  And my tears, as I wept thine own,
But a fairer face thou hast won, love,
  I must weep, I must die, alone!

Or the golden sun had risen,
  Or his mantling essence spread,
The soul had winged its prison,
  The lovely flower was dead!
Or the dew of morn had mounted
  To the home of its second birth,
The tolls of the knell were counted,
  They had laid her in the earth!

A STUDENT'S THOUGHT.

You ask me why I labor thus,
  And why youth's eye should dim with age,
And why I call the night, my day
  To ponder on the painted page.

You say my heart should be as light
  As wont it was in boyhood's days,
If I would cease to be the slave
  Of wisdom and her luring maze.

For all around are cheerful hearts,
    And all around are laughing lips;
Some dancing on the flowery mead,
    Some sailing off on golden ships.

Come, let your books in night repose,
    And lay the weary pen at rest;
Come, come and grace the mystic dance
    And cheer a waiting damsel's breast!

For we remember, comrade dear,
    In days gone by, your merry ways;
No happier voice the chorus joined
    Nor lighter foot was in the race.

We called you king; you could not know
    The confidence you bore away,
The day you left our gleesome band
    To follow learning's golden ray.

But leave your lore, a single night
    To slumber in its gilded tomb;
Come, see the lips you kissed in bud
    And kiss them beautiful in bloom.

" Dear boys! I catch the dreamy clue—
    The past reviving; now my brain
Depicts the glowing photograph,
    And in my youth I live again.

Dear boys! although the ruddy joy
    Of sportive youth has left my cheek,
Although these lips are silent now,
    That, forward once, were wont to speak.

Oh could you force the prison walls
    That hold my heart in servitude,

With deeper, purer love than youth,
   You would behold my heart imbued.

A suffering, sorrowing world has claimed
   My heart to call its treasures in,
That it may have a bounteous store
   To love and lure from sloth and sin.

Oh! could I break the sacred seal
   That holds my lips in silent pain,
A tide of nobler eloquence
   Would make them yours, in youth again!

The veil that o'er my vision steals,
   Some heavenly hand has woven there,
That I may dimly see the earth—
   Its love, pride, anguish, lust, despair!

And could I pierce this sombre shade
   That clouds my vision from your sight,
Far brighter than in days of yore,
   Would beam the glad responsive light.

It glads my soul to see you here!
   I give you now my pledge and word,
I shall forsake the mystic page,
   And we'll renew the broken chord!

And, on the way, to soothe the hour
   And hold our old communion dear,
You'll hear me why I tread that path,
   To you, so destitute of cheer.

This is no age of ghost and dream,
   Nor soul-betraying mystery;
The muses and the fates are dead,
   And gone the spell of prophecy.

But yet unto the faithful mind,
    To life alive, and fired to thought,
Some hopes beyond the present rise,
    Some dreams beyond the present lot.

One night, while I was yet a boy,
    Reposing in my humble bed,
When heaven had set its vigil host,
    And all but thought, undying, dead.

I pondered how my life would run,
    And wondered how I might provide
For the big duties of a man,
    For all the comforts of a bride.

Then deeper sank night's heavy shade,
    And held me close in slumber's arms;
When through the avenues of dream
    Moved an epitome of charms.

She moved within a moving mist
    Of sunlight yellow, as if she
Were wrapt in splendor, to conceal
    A beauty mortal might not see.

But though my heart would barter worlds
    To drink the rapture of those eyes,
To watch the love-inspiring lips,
    That made dark splendor paradise,

Yet, guarded by th' aerial vail,
    The essence of her spirit bright,
She, moving in her gauzy grace,
    Defied the artfulness of sight.

She, bending low, above my sleep
    Just loud enough for heart to hear,

Gave music to my spirit's ear,
   And clothed despair in robes of cheer.

My lips essayed the palsying word,
   But sealed in silence they remained,
Until she broke love's spell with love,
   And with her own, their power unchained.

I murmured soft, "Oh! lovely maid,
   For ever more remain with me,
For love combines no sweeter charms,
   And earth has none so fair as thee!"

Then, from the light-cloud circling her,
   Voluptuous soul-enchanting came,
As from Elysian minstrel poured,
   An eloquence I cannot name.

Its sweetness was the voice of birds,
   Its grandeur was the ocean's roll,
Its transport was the Orphean lyre,
   Its echoes were the curfew's toll.

In fragrant breathings, sweetly sad,
   This strange response she warbled o'er—
"Be true to life, be true to me,
   For I am thine for evermore."

But whither shall I seek a bower
   To plant so fair a virgin-rose,
Or raise wall-barriers heaven-high
   To shield thee from each blast that blows?

And there's no being, sweet enough
   On earth, to be thy waiting-maid,
And *I*—bright lights, look down on *me*,
   For I am wandering in the shade!

My right hand felt a thrilling touch,
  And all my blood was in a race,
To kiss the lucent talisman,
  That stretched beyond the fairy maze.

My arm, my hand remodelled grew,
  As chiselled from the Attic rock;
I gazed, in admiration wild,
  Irrevocable from the shock.

Upon such matchless symmetry,
  Rounded and perfect in its mould,
So white and clear, as to disclose
  The blue life-tide that through it rolled.

" The hero's heart may beat obscure,
  The warrior's blade may rust untried,
The music of the heart may die,
  To heart responsive unapplied.

" But I shall guide thee in thy path;
  I'll turn for thee the book of lore,
And I shall be thyself at death,
  For I am thine for evermore!"

But like an ant that dares a load
  It cannot bear unto its store,
Or shepherd rude, who wins a queen,
  Nor dare he leave her native shore.

Dead-smitten by the pang of love,
  And martyred by relentless shame,
I ventured Scylla's vortex-wave,
  To 'scape the fury of the flame!

I murmured through the muffled gloom
  That vailed the tranquil of repose,

A STUDENT'S THOUGHT.

Half trembling in the hope of love,
    And half convulsed with anger's throes.

Oh! excellence supreme of love,
    Beyond the image of the mind;
The ideal of love's perfect heart,
    And in love's glory-cloud enshrined.

The torture of a frenzied brain,
    The creature of a fleeting dream,
A beacon in the shrouded night,
    Short as the cloud-begotten gleam!

But while the vase of mantling wine
    Shows ruddy in love's festal glow,
I'll drink from sleep's libation, bliss
    That wakeful life must never know.

Then linger near me, lovely maid,
    Though brief the season of my joy,
For soon the dreamless truth of day
    Will night's fair galaxy destroy.

I grieve that day departing brings,
    I grieve that light should thus be rude,
I grieve that consciousness renewed,
    Calls back the voiceless solitude!

The world may have its cynic laugh,
    And hold the dreamer in disdain;
But give to me the dream of bliss
    Before the wakefulness of pain!

"Now, rise the hero of my heart,
    This arm shall wield a mighty sword,
This hand shall mete the numbers out
    That warble to the trembling chord.

"Seek knowledge in the greenwood shade,—
　　Glean wisdom on the lovely shore;
　Go, learn thy music from the wave,
　　For thou art mine forever more!

"Though lorn thy pilgrimage may seem,
　　Involved in gloom, obscured by death;
　My love shall lead thee evermore,
　　My soul incite thee with its breath.

"Take up the banner of the cross,
　　And blazon on its scarlet wing:—
　'To-day the battle I begin,
　　And from the dust shall honor spring'!

"Seize thou the stalwart sword of truth,
　　The pen, the modern king of war,
　And send thy legions trooping forth,
　　Surrounding wisdom's battle-car.

"I, from the flower-embosomed vales,
　　I, from the purple-pillared peaks,
　I, from the living, leaping light,
　　That frets the blue with golden streaks,

"Will garner in the essence, love,
　　To overflowing store my heart,
　That I may speak the mystic tongue,
　　And spell the syllables of art!

"Oh! sweet shall be our evening rest,
　　When I, rejoicing by thy side,
　Shall breathe this treasure-fragrance out;
　　To warm thy numbers with a bride.

"There, as the twilight's tears of dew
　　Glitter in morning's vestal light,

So shall my tiny gems of love
   Give elegance to glorious might.

" How sweetly, when thy task is closed,
   Shall float above th' empurpled mead,
The effluent symphonies of love,
   Embalming nobleness of deed!

" Thy weary head in well-won rest,
   The anvil of thy thought asleep,
How bright shall glow love's shining hearth!
How constant shall love's vigil keep!

" Then, in life's universal sky,
   Reigning all peerless in mid-dome,
Shall hang one liquid golden star,
   And we shall kiss and call it Home."

The drowning sailor, snatched ashore,
   And conscious both of life and death,
Can hear the billows' fatal snore,
   In each reviving draught of breath.

And half he dreads to wake to life
   To know the peril he has passed,
And half he courts the dark abode,
   With shades of night and death o'ercast.

Thus, fettered with the chains of love,
   Incited by its rising star,
I knew the tranquil reign of bliss,
   Endured the passions' stormy war!

When day recalled my life again,
   When conscience had unlocked the mind,
The shadows of the past had flown,
   And light and love my life enshrined.

As if his mission, fate and aim,
   Were but to reach his native sky.

He labors all the pearly day,
   With strong indomitable might;
He weaves his rich enduring web
   Beneath the canopy of night!

Again my energies renew;
   Now love embraces life aglow;
I hear *her* stately footsteps fall;
   The magic of her power I know.

She hangs upon my weary neck,
   With sweetly fairy, gracious art,
And with a confidence sublime,
   She whispers in my listening heart.

Her palm allays my burning brow,
   Soothing the brain with heavenly bliss;
The amaranth of love she lays
   Upon my cheek—a living kiss.

Again I to the battle go,
   Fresh-armed in courage, high with hope,
And with the faithfulness of love,
   With art and hazard bravely cope!

In deep amazement now you ask:—
   "Who haunts your fancy, comrade, thus,
In loyal trust and secresy,
   Unbosom friend, this spell to us."

When I this angel maiden meet,
   Then, soul to soul and life to life,
I'll have her name in heaven writ,—
   The royal name of names,—"My Wife."

He viewed each scene without concern,
And curled his lip in open scorn,—
Enraged by such effectless course,
He rose in vocal accents hoarse.

" Think'st thou, false sorceress, to appal
My spirit with this graven wall,
Or with the bones of this dry frame,
Or with this serpent's eye of flame ?—
Think'st thou the groans of yon dark cell
Can my intrepid soul repel ?
Ha ! no, each but rekindles strife ;
Each fills anew the streams of life !
Time passes like yon bubbling stream—
We see it rippling in the beam ;
But as its waters hurry by,
They fade forever to the eye ;
Nor may we guess what freight may bear
Adown the tide ; we only dare
Behold the fleet when sweeping past,
With swelling sail and giddy mast.
The present lot is ours alone ;
It is our all—the past is gone ;
The future never was, nor is,
Nor ever will be ; it is His
Who, veiled in mystic light, conceals
His greater power, and but reveals
Light adequate unto our need ;
Not our desire demands His meed.
My purpose ? It is wise and brief ;
You are a queen, I am a chief—
You know our warring clans have shed
Their blood like water, and the dead
Lie slumbering upon vale and hill,
Their dust proclaiming vengeance still.
Hear ! should this warfare be prolonged,
Can slaughter gratify the wrong'd ?

SPRING IN THE HEART.

Oh, give my heart a heart to love!
  The little birdies warbling soft
    Are pairing now, and, in light joy,
  They soar and sing to realms aloft:
My heart is sighing, dying, praying;
Burning love meets no allaying—
    Oh, give my heart a heart to love!

Oh, give my heart a heart to love!
  Appease the hunger of its hope;
    Oh, quench its thirstings of desire!
  Bid, bid its vitals cease to mope:
The doves are billing, loving, cooing;
All hearts save mine are wooing, wooing—
    Oh, give my heart a heart to love!

Oh, give my heart a heart to love!
  In love the daisies, violets peep;
    The sun is weeping tears of love,
  And loosed by love the runnels leap:
All nature, love is sanctifying;
Must my poor heart go aching, sighing?
    Oh, give my heart a heart to love!

A STUDENT'S DEATH.

Dead, in the flower of youthful life!
  Dead, my friend, in the morning dew!
Dead to earthly sense and sight—
  Dead, my fellow-struggler true!

"Only a student," the rich man says,
  And a heedless world stands by;

While a thousand hearts of the bravest brand
   Are struggling, loath to die !

The brain keeps burning, burning out,
   In the furnace of its thought ;
And the shadowing wings of darkness broods
   On each jewel of truth begot.

The heart keeps beating, throbbing loud,
   For a heart's response, in vain ;
Till, low and dead, its pulses still,
   In the ruthless grasp of pain.

Oh, hard ! oh, hard is the student's life !
   To barter for morsels of truth,
The hopes of joy, and the light of life,
   And the glorious bloom of youth !

Suffering, sorrowing, battling, praying,
   Dying for love and for light ;
Grinding, worrying, stifling the heart,
   Dying in reaching for right !

Thy earthly task is recited, my friend,
   Thy Master is satisfied :
Enjoy the bliss of the blest, dear friend,
   The rest of the sanctified !

Dear friend, thy seekings for truth are o'er,
   For the Truth now stands revealed—
The Truth which the soil and the lust of earth
   From thy eager eye concealed.

Dear friend, thy gropings for light are o'er,
   For the Light of eternal day
Now leads thy soul through the gates of heav'n,
   With its holy, incarnate ray.

Thy strugglings for life are o'er, dear friend,
    The secret pang, hope's tear;
For thou art enshrined in immortal life,
    Free from regret and fear.

Oh, spirit of him who toiled so hard
    For the student's lofty goal!
Send out a beam of thy truth and light
    To illumine the student's soul!

That he may not wreck on the hidden rocks,
    On the quicksands of despair,
While the homes and the hearts are closed and deaf
    To the cry of the student's prayer!

Over the sleep of thy youthful heart
    A blossom of fame shall grow;
Over thy grave shall a brother soul
    Water it with his woe.

Onward I press for the distant prize
    Which thou hast won so young;
Upward I move for the golden crown
    Which glory has over thee flung.

TO A LADY WEEPING.

    Fair lady, rise;
Nor let the briny, scalding tear
Course its red channel on those features dear,
    Give love no sacrifice.

    Dost see yon velvet cloud
Bathing its dark, airy tresses
In liquid glory, in bright heaven's caresses,
    Robed with a sapphire shroud?

    See, in the blue, blue heaven,
It glides voluptuously along,
Revelling in joy—its sweetly silent song
    Discoursing—to angels given.

    'Tis silent now and airy,
Now like a blood-red banner—now
Kingly purple—azure—gold—its brow
    And form change as a fairy!

    O dear one, that is love
How lofty! heavenly! but how fleeting!
That cloud thy theme is now repeating.
    Yon is the poet's turtle dove.

    See, now how dark
It grows, as night had plumed her sable wing,
And veiled the secrets of the starry ring,
    Now it dissolves, hark!

    Ah! the gloomy rain!
The cloud was love—these are love's tears,
The fruit of joys, of hopes, of sighs and fears!
    O love is *pain!*

THE SAILOR'S GRAVE.

LET the warrior sleep in his martial mail,
    With his iron-heart untrammelled;
Let him sleep on the hill where the hero fell,
    With the light of fame enamelled;
But lay me to rest where the billows toil,
    Where the waves, in dark devotion,
Roll up in their glorious, furious strength,
    From the breast of the briny ocean!

Ho! ho! let the sea, in its frantic glee,
  Break my sleep, in its wild commotion!

Let the pilgrim sleep on the foreign shore,
  That his friends may dream in sorrow,
That their loved one comes from the golden clime,
  To illumine their dark to-morrow;
But let my slumbers broken be
  By the groans of the dying billow;
Let me sleep in the shroud of the azure wave,
  And the white sea-sand my pillow—
Where the murmurs low of the wavelet's throe
  Make vocal the soughing willow!

'Twas there that my heart, in boyish dreams,
  Sent ships to the isles of glory;
'Twas there that my daring manhood stemmed
  The pride of the mountains hoary;
'Tis there that she sleeps, my heart of hearts,
  In the sleep that knows no breaking,
With a blue-eyed babe on her throbless breast,
  Love, in death, still unforsaking!
Ho! ho! let me lie where the billows cry,
  In the sleep that knows no waking!

HECTOR AND ALICE.

(A Story of Queenston.)

AUTUMN had rolled his chariot o'er the earth,
With flaming sceptre searing nature's breast,
Till, in slow death of hopeless combat, she
Resigned her blooming children to despair;
And ever, as the war-prince marshalled on,
His path was strewn with laurels of their pride,
Now, the crisp toys of air. 'Twas afternoon;
The sweetly halcyon sky stooped down to weep;
The earth was tranquil as a child's repose;
The forest, like a queen, with crownless brow,
Stood in the mingled splendor of her state,
And veiled her bosom's palpitating throes,
Beneath a sombre tracery of boughs,
In fulgent majesty, the sun, on earth,
Wept down his copious tears of liquid gold;
The river, wandering waveless, murmured on,
Its foam the dance of red and yellow leaves.
But, round the borders of our land beloved,
Closed dark th' eclipsing wings of tyranny;
And, as a cloud that swamps the morning star,
Menaced the freedom of our embryo life;
Till, true to each proud mem'ry of the past,
Each glowing impulse of the loyal heart,
Beating indignant the full swell of life,
She, like Achilles incensed, took the field,
And let the tempest of ingenuous wrath
Burst the vile chains that would enthral the free.

While thus, convulsively, war's fiery tide
Surged in huge billows in our country's breast,

A tall, lithe maiden stood upon the shore
Of Erie's silent deep. Down her fine form,
Flowed silken elegance of jetty hair
Waving around her snowy brow, as play
The azure ripples of the stranded wave
Along the margin of the white sea sand.
Full of the eloquence of love, her eyes
Were like the splendor of the darkest night,
With pensive Luna reigning in mid-dome.
Upon the lilied tablets of her cheek,
Flourished the rosy pink of virtuous youth.
Silent she stood, with all the slumberous depth
Of the still sea, reflected in her face;
As if, a sprite from deep, green-pillared cell,
Her over-curious soul had lured away;
While, she, unconscious, waited its return.
Pain, mingled with the wistfulness of hope,
Grief, gazing at high-barriered bliss, were there;
There, love, in holy adoration wrapt
In voiceless language, symbolized her trust.

With sudden joy, the lips awoke, "Hector!"
With light, ecstatic, fawn-like bound, she clasp'd
His neck, and pressed his heart to hers;
Then her impulsive power relaxing, she
Gazed in glad wonderment into his eyes,
Exclaiming, "Dauntless Hector hast thou come!"

He spoke no answer; but, with saddest smile,
Held her before admiring, till, she, grown
In fear, distrustful of her sight, said, "speak,
My darling! for my thirsty heart now craves
The mantling potions of thy love. Last night
I dreamt, that, having left that land, Hector,
That would oppress us now, thou stood'st, my king,
Before me thus; but ere I could embrace
Thee, thou had'st fled, leaving me dream-betray'd,

And, wandering aimlessly unto this beach
I stood and pictured thee upon the wave;
And asked my heart, oh! will thy hero come?
Oh! shall I be his bride on Christmas Day?
Whereat my blood came pulsing from its fount
Anew, whilst I could feel the hectic toil
That made my brain reel hot. But forward then,
As Neptune conjured from the sleeping deep,
To chide my bosom's terrors hast thou come
Oh! speak sad-love!"
      He, disengaging, stood
A moment in the consciousness of strength;
Then, with the bravery of love, pressed back
Unto his hungry heart, his promised bride;
And, radiant in her raptured light, replied :—
" Alice, far from that stranger land I've come,
Remindful of that double-loyal pledge
That links my heart to thine, likewise
My strength and honor to my native land;
But, darling, this is not the hour for words,
Suffice it now that Hector loves, and true
To every bond of love that holds us one;
But it doth pierce me, for thy sake, to think
What dangers fill our land!"
       She sprang away,
And, kneeling on the sands, clasp'd her white hands,
Expressing piteously, " Oh! Hector, go
Not to the war, lest my poor dream be true
In joy and grief."
     " Alice," he said, " arise
Behold, while we in converse join, the sky
Has called her myriad sons to battle! See
The sun has wandered into darkness dead!
Lo! from the stilly bosom of the deep
Uprear the black-brow'd giants trooping forth!
Dark are these heralds, oh, my love, but true.
Thus would th' aggressor, destitute of cause,

Roll the black shroud of ignominious death
Around our land; and as those gloomy sons
Of ocean sally forth against the wall
Of adamantine rock, the foe would sweep
The hurricane of death around our homes.
But, as that rock, shall we repel their wrath,
And send them shattered to their native depths.
No foe's invading foot shall stamp reproach
Upon the soil our fathers' blood has bought—
No desecrating tyrant shall impose
That bondage that our sires have taught to spurn—
No sacrilegious scorn shall stain our shrines,
Dear homes, inviolable hearts—truth's throne,
Till the last spark of fire shall languish dead,
Till the last drop of life shall cease to run,
In the last heart of Canada's brave sons;
When, vanquished, they shall sleep immortally!
Arise, my love, and with thy noblest kiss,
Speed me to fight. The bugle sounds. Arise!
The hero of Detroit, the gallant Brock,
Is marching to the thunder-throated strait,
I follow him,—tumultuous is the night,—
VanRansellaer will cross amid the dark,
Unless we place immediate sentry on.
Fear not for me, sweet Alice, I shall live,
And Christmas morn shall toll our marriage bells.
Pray, bear all bravely, praying for this land,
And victory for the arms defending Right."
Then, mounting far above each weaker part,
She rose composed, and heroic in power,
And giving him that blessed boon—a kiss,
She said, "God bless thee, Hector, to the field!"

Forward in the great form of war, they march;
Steep hill-sides scaling, threading labyrinths
Of rugged mounts, thence plunging into dark,
Profound ravines, and merging into wild

Entanglements of virulent morass,
Through furrow'd fields to ebon night again.
From every home kept watch the wakeful film;
No slumber soothed these homes; for night,
By lethal fear, robbed of its balminess,
Was only blacker day. The watch dog heard
The heavy thunder of the soldiers' march
And, through the gloom, sent his portentous howl.
Its dread alarm the fearful night-bird screamed.
Foremost, in this herculean march of fate,
Was Hector. He knew well the pathless woods,
And where dark stream took birth, or precipice
Yawned deep. He, as a pilot leading on
His fleet, cheered from disaster with his skill.
Till, as the midnight moon, involved in clouds,
In thirteenth passage through October skies,
Had climbed the arch to its meridian throne,
The guardian champions of a loyal land
Stood for the fight before the toiling wave!

All night, as Hector sentried on the beach,
Dark floods lashed the invulnerable rock,
Their foaming rage retreating with a wail;
Whilst, overhead, Vulcan's great sword of flame
Cleft the deep gloom with sudden sweep; till low
And moaning in the distance, burst the peal
Of rolling thunder on the trembling earth.
Now, intermittent with the clashing groans
Of elemental ire, could Hector feel
The blood of his strong, princely youth rush full
And fitful, as retiring wave forsook,
With weird remorse, the high embattled coast,
That seemed the muttered undertone of war
To herald foe from o'er the boiling gorge.
Then he would firmly grapple sword and halt,
Peering intently o'er the ebon flood.
Composed again, he thought his country's weal,

And Alice Bond, weening he ever heard
Her say, "God bless thee, Hector, to the fight!"

Aurora, pale and wakeful, from her couch,
Beheld the foe creep like a stealthy snake,
From the bleak rocks, and slide into the stream.
"To arms!" cried Hector; and, the bivouac,
Roused from brief slumber, marshalled in array,
The martial music ardently appealed;
True loyalty beat high in every breast;
Down poured the volley on th' invading souls,
Till as dry leaves in the tornado's whirl,
Shivered, they drove headlong before the storm!
Up rose the free-born victor-shout. But lo!
On yonder hill rearward, our sullen guns
Lost in a darkly surging mass—the foe!
Raising his brow towards heaven, Brock exclaimed,
"Our guns are captured! Follow me, Brave Boys!"
And charged against the hill. That was the hour
When heroes proved their valor, loyalty;
That was the hour when Glory crowned our sons!
Be proud of them, Young Canada! For thee
They fought, for thee they died, they won for thee!
They sleep! they sleep! Young Canada! and, though
No earthly honor marks their graves, there, Love,
Truth, Worth, Faith, Victory and Gratitude
Of a young nation's hopes and joys are set!
The brightest page by Glory chronicled
Upon the records of our rising fame
Is his, who quenched the golden star of life,
And sank immortal in a hero's grave!

Our hero, Hector, all that day of blood,
While up that hill, invincible as Death,
Our valiant scions charged th'unwavering rock
Of fortitude above, while Queenston heard
A thunder louder than th' incessant roar

That guards her portals, stern unconquerably,
Amongst the brave, moved Titan-like and first
In the forefront, amidst the sleet of fate.
'Twas not, till Sheaffe, outgeneralling the foe,
At bayonet's point, drove left to right, and wheeled
His desperate legions up against the mass,
And headlong hurled it o'er the precipice,
That Hector, wounded sore in head and heart
Despising pain, in grim reluctance, fell.
But ere his senses ventured Lethe's tide,
One quick exultant rally back to life
They made, as upward to the welkin, rang
The proud, impulsive pæan of the free !

Unconscious as the dead, among the dead
He lay. The gatherers of the wounded said,
" He sleeps," and left him lying with the dead ;
Until a tearful mother, daring near,
Low weeping in her sympathy of grief,
Hearing the faintest echo of a sigh,
In Hector's breast, found yet a spark alive.
She was a widow, and her darling son
Had perished in the darling cause of right ;
And nursing Hector's feeble vital-lamp,
And watching every flicker of its flame,
And dressing daily his slow-healing wounds,
And whispering sweet in his unconscious ear,
She learned to love him as her own ; and poured
Above him many a faithful prayer, or sang
Some lowly whispering hymn fraught with the past,
Till Love and Sorrow, Pity and Regret,
Would crowd her mind, and speak in tears.

Ten times, the monarch of the day had troop'd
His golden warriors o'er the azure hill,
And Alice stood again upon the beach.
The sand was smooth and hard, the pebbles white,

Crisp, crinkling leaves played gambols with her feet.
She mused impatient; and, dishevelled some,
Her raven hair hung loose, Her lustrous eye
Had dimmed its brilliancy; while, from her cheek,
Had paled the rosy pink of bloomy youth.
While pensive thus she mused, a tall, dark youth,
Emerging, strode from out the dreaming woods,
With warm familiar smile saluting her :—

" My own adored, my loved one, Alice Bond !
Here, on this mossy trunk, where autumn hath
Placed his soft footstep, sweet with nature's balm,
Rest at my side, and hear love's plaintive voice.
I've longed to meet thee ; I have longed
To breath a word, a precious word."

" Oh, Roger, be not harsh ! call me not names
That, coming from thy lips, unholy sound,—
Names that one human soul alone may call—
Names that God's angels witness once for each !
I'll sit beside thee, Roger, my good friend,
My true, old friend, my *friend, only* my *friend:*
In daring further, you will favor less.
Yes ! Roger, sit, and give my aching heart
Some old forgotten tale to wake its throb ;
For oh ! the biting pain of prescient dread
That clouds the vision of my ardent hope,
And clips of holy faith its heaven-plumed wings,
To nothingness keeps pressing in my life !

The happy leaves have fallen from the trees,
And, from my heart, has died the blossom-hue ;
The birds are weeping valedictory songs ;
My soul's last melodies are echoing.
In farewell smile, the year is blushing now ;
And I am dying, dying in my love."

"Be not so fearful. Life o'erteems with love.
Hope shines co-eval with the human heart.
They sear a little in the autumn frost,
But spring to them perennial bloom revives.
The heart a weak thing seems; what mighty loads
It shoulders. Though the weakest instrument
In love, it is the sturdiest in life.
What though the lily's softly parted lips
Receives no more Eolus' sensuous kiss!
What though not now, among the bright green grass,
The violets peep with starry, purpled eye!
What though entrancing spells the forest hold!
Who cares to know how silly songsters pipe?
If nature sleep, we'll have a gala day;
So, cheer up! love give ear:—'Is not my heart
More worth to thee, than elements of earth?
Be mine dear Alice! from the radiant morn,
As constant as the sun in his long course,
Till stars shall light the day into repose,
For thee, my hands shall toil nor ever tire.
Of nothing but thy weal my brain shall think;
My heart—oh take it—it shall rear aloft,
For thy abode, a temple golden-walled.
Its windows shall be diamonds pinken, blue,
With their pellucid water for the panes,
So that no light save that of innocence
Shall touch thy orb. The guardian emerald,
That doth contemn all hate, shall be the door,
That Truth and Trust alone be our great guests.
Of blessed pearl the cornices shall form;
The floor of agate patines shall be paved,
That in imperishable peace we walk,
The bloodless sapphire, ruby violet,
The soul-composing amethyst, shall shine
Corruscent, on the orient-pinioned roof.
In graceful majesty, shall stand the clean
Corinthian columns of jaspidean sheen,

With chapiters of peerless chrysolite;
While music's zephyrs shall aroma steal
From every blossom of immortal love,
Softly instilling in thy dream of life,
Elysian fragrance, love-diffused! My dear,
May I not call thee mine? My Alice Bond?"

"Oh Roger, friend, forbear! My heart—My heart
Is breaking! Roger, well I know thy wealth;
For California has, to thee, unlocked
Her golden-cinctured treasury. But oh!
In earthly deeps, there is not wealth enough,
The issues of one heart to counterweigh,
The heart fastidious is in choice of fare;
Its appetite can relish nought but love.
Go, Roger, to some maid of high estate;
For thou art worthy of earth's truest heart;
Woo *her*; bow down, and at her dainty feet,
Kindle, upon the crystal shrine of love,
The gilded sacrifice of opulence,
Discourse to me to-day, old times and ways;
Of faithful friends departed, dead, relate,
Of days of innocence and mirth gone by,
Of thy wild wand'rings in the dreary west,
Of those, who, in the quest of gold, met death;
Or let our converse touch this present war,—
Haply e'en now our valiant hearts go down,
I'm much amazed that in this hour of peril,
Thy might and chivalry should linger here,—
Speak at thy will, but do not ask my heart
It is too feverish for pensive toil!"

"With best relief to thy great wonderment,
Revealment of all causes I shall make.
That I am here despite my country's need,
Speaks not, dear Alice, lack of loyalty,
But here I stand to battle for myself,

That better I may soldier for my land.
Against the castle of thy heart, I hold
My siege. That won, I'm emperor of fate.
Pray one brief word forgive, Alice divine,—
My wealth alone I proffer not ; my heart
Is postured first. If dubious shadows rise,
As to the sterling of allegiance vow'd,
Bid me leap into everlasting sleep,
Beneath the fathoms of those billows blue ;
I shall ! This passion is no moment's bloom ;
Together we were school'd ; thou knowest me ;
Knowest thou dishonor, wantonness, deceit,
Attainting the fair record of my life ?
From childhood, ere the wayward heart could read
The language of its own wild song, I loved ;
And with the manhood of my strength and form,
To sovereign perfectness my love attained.
Say that thou lovest,—give me thy white hand,—
And I shall tell thee tales of quaint romance,
And sing thee songs of lovely melody,
Until the red-pavillioned monarch, Day,
His quenchless overflowing glory-orb
Has to a dead cold cinder languished !
That stuff, termed wealth, deem not an obstacle.
I've seen the sun shine in a hundred lands ;
A hundred tongues observed the soul discourse ;
In all, I find life is one changeless theme.
The soul is ever groping for the light,
Downward to slide the man is ever prone ;
Ever some hope-star lights the clouded eye ;
While, through the wiles environing the life,
The glorious prince, called mind,—God's self
In lesser measure manifest in man,
To victory is ever triumphing.
Around the planet, life is life, no more ;—
A common medley of various parts ;
Aims, purposes, remorses, hopings, griefs,

Joys, sins, regrets, ambitions, strugglings,—
A time-long wrestle for autocracy,
Among a thousand riotous, old heirs!
Among my gleanings, I've red-lettered this,
That, when the heart is dolorous, no power,
Nor pageantry; no dignity, nor wealth;
Can minister. The heart, alone, can cure
The heart. Solon's was true philosophy;
Lydia's King was *poor*. The happiest men,
The men who daily live to toil, to toil
That they may live. For them, to love is life.
E'en here, among conflicting elements,
There is a smile, that lucre cannot claim,
A touch of hands, too sanctified for wealth,
A loyal kiss, so wrapt in purity,
That angels, on soft wings, to heav'n bear it,
A love-formed tear, God's sacrifice to man.
Oh, Alice! think not of my wealth. Be mine!
I'll lay it all, at pleasure of thy will,
Bless thou the poor, and make me almoner;
Or build a hospital, where I may dwell;
For, in disdaining my regards, thou shalt,
A deeper fall than Vulcan's was, give me
My bellows other far than his may be
I shall be crippled hopelessly! ah me!"

"As fair, Roger, art thou, unto my eye,
As noble, gentle, true as any man;
And lest that truth indwelling thee so strong,
Should mispronounce my sad, sad constancy,
Deeming me fortified in rude disdain,
Because I hold thee as a gentle friend,
True to thyself, and therefore to all true.
I'll tell thee Roger why I cannot love;
And yet, I may not, for this prescient heart,
So full of wailing and far requiem bells,
At any breath may close its rosy gates.

Had'st thou been long returned, good Roger Lang,
Thou had'st become familiar with this theme.
I need not quest thee, Roger, dost thou know
Our mutual, old school-fellow, Hector Wade;
For many a dewy, summer morn, I've sat
Watching you both, in your Olympic sport,—
God bless his valor on the field of war,
To day he may have sterner games to play!—
I need not more relate,—my heart is his;
Nor if I could, would I recall it now."

"I hold it, Alice Bond, most hazardous
To life and piety, to thus embody all
Your love and hope, in one uncertain man."

"Say not, 'uncertain,' Roger, would'st thou yet
Enjoy the friendship lately pledged in trust;
Though errantly the stars through space should swim,
Apollo cease to ride his golden car,
The wing'd evangelists forget to bear,
Of High Omnipotence the heraldings,
In Hector Wade, my trust should stay unsoiled!"

"My lovely Alice, pardon I beseech!
Nor think, that for a thousand worlds, would I,
Across his spotless name, cast one small shade:
I spoke not of uncertainty of heart,
But accident. Full well, Alice, you know,
We all are toys upon the tide of fate.
May Hector, valorous, invincible,
Not sink beneath the thunder-stone of war?
Where then could all thy faith and love divine
Find anchor on the shoreless ocean-world?"

"There is one harbor still for stately crafts,
Whose gates are wide and open as the world;—
The gate is Death; the harbor is the grave;
There would I moor my melancholy life!"

" Not mine to disavow sincerity,
Or play the cynic with affection's truth;
For, in such prudency doth candor robe,
And in fidelity there is such worth,
That dare not folly, pride, deceit gainsay;
Earth, notwithstanding, hedges every hope
With circumstance, condition, dubiousness.
Where thus the aimings of desire take flight,
Beyond the jurisdiction of desire,—
The finite leaping to the infinite—
Why should the life we have be bartered off
For that we cannot have, which, if possessed,
In avarice, itself would dispossess?
Supernal seems the purple arras-vail
Of eve; but, like a banner glory-stain'd,
Is rolled away,—we love it not the less;
For morn, with wak'ning kiss, shall dry
The clear, cold tears of love-forsaken earth;
And from the mount-tops, breathing golden light,
Warm to a blush the pallid cheek asleep;
So all things die; and, from their dust, arise
Of better things, the embryo essences.
Hector is worthy of thy love; therefore
Let loyal love be his empyrean light;
But rein, by the strong hand of will, and hold
In circumscription of thy reason fair,
The ardency and urgency of love;
So come the bitterest decree of fate
Against the cherished languor of thy faith,
A margin for the aftermath remains.
It is not noblest life that lavishes,
On every venture its entire resource.
Should Hector Wade, to thee, return no more,
Our sympathy shall mingle mutual tears,
For sorrow is as valorous as love.
Then summon thy reserve of fortitude;
And rally to the rescue of thy life.

I will instal me thy knight-banneret,
And wage eternal feud with circumstance"
"Go Roger Lang, forbear persistence rude,
In harrowing thoughts, that whisper death to me.
To me, thy hard philosophy is vain ;
I love my Hector ! How could I retain
A mite of love, far insufficient all,
A thousand hearts had I, instead of one ;
And each, a thousand fold, were magnified ;
And all love's fountain gates, ajar were thrown ;
These, were as little rivers, gambolling
To the vast ocean of his love.   True love
All pain doth sanctify ; to sorrow breathe
A balm—departing earth, exultingly
It mounts to heaven !
    Oh ! Roger Lang, if thou
Dost love me, leave me here to solitude ;
For though, from the Elysian-lighted realms,
An angel whispered to me, 'Hector dies ;'
I could not then thy proffered hand accept."
"Be not impulsive in thy votive zeal,
My darling Alice.   When the thing that *seems*,
Becomes what *is*, a new complexion oft
Is stamped upon our articles of faith ;
And, he, who dreams to make his weakness strong
By resolutions violently sworn,
Finds in the siege his battlements but straw.
From out the gloom permit one ray to shine
Dear Alice—"
    " Roger, I shall never yield
To be a traitor in the least degree.
Some rash distemper of both head and heart
Must sway your honor from its sober will,
Farewell !"
    " Stay, Alice ! I am not myself.
But has your mind not ferreted the cause ?
Stay, Alice, stay, God bless you, Alice stay !

Oh, that your love for Hector were less firm!"
In dark amaze she stood; while Roger bent,
Wringing his tearful brow; and brokenly
Expressed, "Oh, Alice, I am from the war!"

Her parted lips made vain essay to speak;
She trembled once, then petrified remained.
Then Roger Lang's dark brow did darker grow;
As under sad compulsion he must speak.
"Alice," he said, and ceased to check a sob,
" I was brave Hector's comrade all through life;
We were twin-brothers in each purpose, act;
And, I was with him to the last, and came
To tell you how he died!" here, Alice gave
A light, incredulous, half-sighing laugh.
Proceeding, Roger told her, how they fought;
How dauntless Hector braved the battle-tide;
And, how he wounded fell; concluding with—
His last words were,—' now Roger, we two part!
My country's saved! I'm wounded to the heart!
Speed on and leave me here; for, I can die
Alone! your country calls your aid! Farewell!
But Roger ere I die,'—and from his breast
Thy miniature he drew, and blessed and kissed,
—' Oh tell my loving Alice, how I died;
Constant to her, till death! Roger, farewell!'
The fight was raging, I, compelled to go;
But, in the twilight silent, wandered back,
But could discover not dear Hector there,
Nor in the hospital! Some nameless grave
Holds the brave heart in Glory's tranquil sleep!"

Her vision now, in clouds, became obscured;
Thick gloom, around her half unconscious soul,
Brooded; Life was a rayless shadow-land;
Her skiff was drifting, drifting o'er the tide,
With sails set full expectant; but the shore,

Receding, mocked the eager prow. Long, long
In anguish, hope, despair, she pulled amain
The dim beguiling strand to make, for there
Stood Hector, beckoning with siren voice !
At length, she struck the marge : Hector had fled ;
A new creation laughed at her distress ;
Hard, unfamiliar voices greeted her ;
Upon her, frowned eyes human, dead to love ;
Youth seemed a child, and yet had furrow'd cheek ;
Sounds had dark import ; fitful tempests roared ;
Young twilight never set in night, or burn'd
To day ; action was fraught with mystery.
Thus, through the shadowy wood, and up the hill,
Red with the life-blood of the trees, she sped,
Weaving her plaint, in echoes weird and sad !

Meanwhile, near the dark border-land of death,
Unconscious of the busy ebb and flow
Of circumstance, lay Hector Wade, unknown.
But, even in oblivion's gloomy cell,
He had his little world,— a home and love ;
For Alice, moving in a golden mist
Which half-concealed identity, was there.
Thus, slowly convalescent rose his strength ;
And Life's blue streams that had been drainèd dry,
Drop after drop, replenished their low wave ;
While his faint energies, with growing beat,
Rallied around the monarch of their throne.
But though his vigor and his vital throb
Themselves restored, his mind seemed vacant still.
His eye was not magnetic to response,
But cold and lightless as a marble mome.
Like strong Achilles, from fair Briséis.
By wily Agammemnon's wrath withheld,
He pined in dark unutterable woe,—
A dream of death that knew no wakening,
Changeless, they bore him to that awful tomb !

Where Reason's ray but flickers, as the light
Of an undying day shoots in between
The metal bars that guard its cheerless night.
Wherein, long sleepless nights and days unblest,
In blank and sullen vacancy of mind,
Upon his soul's epitome he pored,
Not breaking with a sigh, dread solitude.

Bright Christmas morn! Refulgent rose the sun;
And, from his glowing brow, diffused to air,
And earth in marriage splendor white,
The yellow essence of resplendent light.
The voice, with mellow sweetness was intoned,
As, when two friends, long parted, meet again,
Above the lily-pillow'd sleep of death.
The eye was full of fascinating love;
Warm, radiant, life-transpiercing light.
Poured from the soul, the man immaculate;
The face, with gladness gloriously subdued,
Asked for a kiss to warm its sacred shrine;
Bursting with joy, that comes from doing good,
The heart did flutter up against its cage,
Eager to try its lightning wings abroad;
The world set sail beyond the land of toil,
For its great school was loose for holiday;
Youth and youth's love were vowing love,
And like the rhyme of fancy rang the bells;
Light-hearted children, angels of the earth,
Were shouting "Merry Christmas" laughingly;
But, in the home of Richard Bond, where joy
Should set the nuptial torch aflame, was grief!
Then rose a feeling, tenderest of earth,
The mother, pensive, heavy-hearted, said:—
"Dear Richard, let us go and see our child,
And try and comfort her poor lonely heart.
I'll bring along some Christmas gifts,
This pretty ottoman, some Christmas cards,

And golden ink, that she may write her name;
Likewise the silken, vestal white trousseau,
For it may please her; she may wish it on!
Poor Hector's mother shall accompany;
She longs to see her darling daughter, too."

Reclining on a crimson-gilded couch,
They Alice found, dressing her glossy hair.
They spoke to her, suppressing tears with smiles;
And gave her all their pretty Christmas gifts.
She sighed, then gave a wild, hysteric laugh,
The darkly-purpled, brilliant ottoman
She placed herself upon; and, on the cards,
Traced with the lustrous flowing liquid pen;—
"Poor Hector Wade! On Christmas he will come!"
Then trilled a simple monody, ending;—
"Yes! Christmas morn shall toll our marriage bells,"
Now, as rang out the sweet cathedral bells,
With quick impatience rousing, she enquired,—
"What bells are ringing?" Meeting this response,
"The Christmas chimes, my daughter, my fair child."
"Oh, haste!" she cried, "and in my marriage robes
Array me! for my Hector comes to-day!"
"Oh! my dear child," her mother answered her,
"Your gallant Hector fell among the slain;
Nor can he come to wed fair Alice Bond!
He sleeps,—oh! death to all our hopes,—in death."
"Oh, you are strangers!" Alice made reply;
"You do not know my Hector's daring love!
But get me in my marriage gown, I say;
For Christmas morn shall toll our marriage bells!"
They, to appease her errant fancy-dream,
Arrayed her in her beauteous wedding robes;
In golden bands they placed the lily wrists;
On her translucent finger set a ring;
They crowned her bosom with the Persian gem,
A gemmy coronet adorned her brow.

"Now to the bridal altar lead me forth !
The bridegroom waits, my king, my lord, for me !"
Across the threshold, to the long arcade,
They led her, like a stately stepping queen.
Passing along, they found some doors ajar,
For the humane of heart remembered, this
Was Christmas Day ; and Hector's sullen mood
Being all innocuous, he was left at will.
As, pale and silent, sat he gazing dead
Upon his life-sustaining talisman,
With weirdly wand'ring eyes, reclaiming light,
And lips that faltered words unspeakable.
A moment, Alice stood at Hector's door,
Exclaiming in her new-found ecstacy,
"My lord ! my king ! my noble Hector Wade !"

As, at the touch of Auster's balmy breath,
The hermit of the frozen rocks, awakes
In glad amazment from his half-year's sleep,
To view new beauty throned upon the earth,
So Hector, at the thrilling voice of love,
Awoke and cast aside his Lethean chains ;
His every part was perfect consciousness
Again ; the thousand strings in unison.
The mind, restored to fallen sovereignty,
Sedition had subdued by its ukase !
"My Alice !" Royal Reason's light returned ;
Restored to Love's white brow its queenly crown.
Within each other's arms, their lives embraced,
And Christmas Day did consecrate them one !

CANADIAN HYMN.

While Freedom's white banner shall reign the ascendant,
   While Honor defendeth the cause of the brave,
While Love, Truth and Justice, in emblems resplendent,
   Embattle the empire, and beacon the wave,
Go forward, in triumph, strong sons of the forest,
   Hope's star and the lily of peace on each breast;
Your sea-circled garden embellish with labor;
   Glad homes be her valleys, from east to the west!

From where blue Atlanta ariseth in splendor,
   To where the dark waves of Superior sleep,
May Canada boast that her heroes defend her,
   And, nurtured to glory, her vigil stars keep,
No parasite weeds round her pillars of glory,
   By brave hearts protected, and braver hearts won;
No traitor's affection shall tarnish the story,
   That, down the long ages, in glory, shall run!

But should war's angel unfold his red herald,
   Command its loud thunder awaken our shore;
Should the warm hearts of our loves be imperilled,
   Or tyrant dishonor the shrines we adore;
Set round your heart, like a halo of glory,
   All the dear gems of your country and home;
Gird on the armor of Right, Truth and Honor,
   Fight,—fight, till, immortal, you conquer your doom!

SONG OF THE CRADLE.

Poets have sung of the bed and the bier;
   Soldiers exalted the sword and the spear;
Children have worshipped the nurse and the knee;
   But none have thought worthy to eulogize me;—

Rock-a-way, rock-a-away, all the long day;
  Through the dark night I am rocking away.

People may deem me unworthy of fame;
  And try to reprove me of folly and shame;
But I've codled them all, as shortly you'll see,
  No—I never rock'd *Adam*—but he has rocked *me*;—
Rock-a-way, rock-a-way all the long day;
  Through the dark night I am rocking away.

Ah! well I remember, how Eve looked and smiled,
  As I lulled to reposing her beautiful child;
And fondly I reckoned a patron in Cain,
  But he was bad one,—I reckoned in vain;—
Rock-a-way, rock-a-way all the long day;
  Through the dark night I am rocking away.

Although my first nursling thus brought me disgrace,
  Pray think not this hard of the whole of my race;
Be not hypercritical; think of yourself,
  And thousands far better long laid on the shelf !—
Rock-a-way, rock-a-way all the long day;
  Through the dark night I am rocking away.

I've nursed all the poets, to sweeten their bliss,
  I've endowed the rude lispers with hug and with kiss,
Confiding in hoping that when they'd grow old,
  My virtues they'd sing and my history be told;
But then, quite forgetting my labor of love,
  They sang of the star, of the rose and the dove;
Of heroes and lovers; of martyrs and wars;
  Of silly young maidens; of Venus and Mars;—
Rock-a-away, rock-a-away all the long day;
  Through the dark night, I am rocking away.

I'm clear independent of preacher or bard;
  My hours they are long, and my pathway is hard.

I'll chide, when I please ; for they dare not stop me ;
  I have *this* consolation,—I'm rocking away ;—
Rock-a-away, rock-a-away all the long day ;
  Through the dark night I'm rocking away.

They talk about muses ! The muses are mine ;
  And, tuck'd in my flannel, they safely recline.
Bless me ! in their haughtiness, poets forget
  I taught them their metre by rocking the beat.
Yes ! I've heard them, ere now, singing songs to the child,
  That I taught to themselves or they ever were styled ;
I have heard them applauded as noble and wise,
  For rhymes, I inspired, ere they opened their eyes ;—
Rock-a-way, rock-a-way all the long day ;
  Through the dark night, I am rocking away.

I'm not at all jealous. I wish them all well ;
  But thus, by compulsion, my story I'll tell.
I've waited too long ; and, I'll wager my flock,
  That the poet, who writes, shall have plenty to rock ;—
Rock-a-way, rock-a-way all the long day ;
  Through the dark night, I am rocking away.

I don't wish to flatter ; but I'll tell you the truth ;
  I've enjoyed the best company all through my youth,
I have shaken the hand of the wit and the sage ;
  I've laughed at their humor, and scowled at their rage,
The world calls them angels. I can't understand
  How mankind can idolize such a rude band !
Come with me, to the study, the hall and the bath,
  And you'll swear they *are* angels, but angels of *wrath* ;
Rock-a-way, rock-a-way all the long day ;
  Through the dark night, I am rocking away.

If I'm not just as innocent as I *should* be,
  It is that I've mingled with humanity ;

So good folks be kindly. Remember with dread,
  Your *secrets*, I know. Do you wish them all spread ?
Rock-a-way, rock-a-way all the long day ;
  Through the dark night, I am rocking away.

" GOOD-BYE."

(In three parts.)

FORTUNE cold has frowned upon me ;
  I have tried to act the man ;—
Many a day, I've prayed and struggled,
  Till my youthful cheek is wan :
'Twas for you, my loved, my darling,
  That I bore the pang and sigh ;
But, my every effort failing,
  I have come to say, " Good-bye."

I am all unworthy of you ;
  But your loving bade me raise
All my thoughts to noble aimings,
  All my soul to heavenly praise :
In despair, you fonder loved me ;
  Soothed with kisses every sigh,—
Love ! I'm all unworthy of you,—
  I have come to say " Good-bye."

To a distant land I'll wander ;
  Wander ? No ; thy love shall lead,
And thy image shall inspire me,
  To all nobleness of deed.
Dearest ! soul of my existence,
  Will you love me still, if I
Shall return to claim my treasure ?
  Kiss me love and say " Good-bye."

THE ANSWER.

Roses bloom in every valley,
   Still unknown to human eye ;
Dark may be the day and dreary,
   But the sun shines in the sky :
'Tis the field that tries the soldier ;
   Life's hard battles make great men,—
Good-bye, with my love's warm blessing !
   We shall gladly meet again.

He that dares to mount the billow
   Of life's darkly surging sea,—
He that with his fate dare falter,
   One day holds the golden key
Thou art worthy of *all* honor,—
   Life and love are joy and pain—
Thou art worthier now than ever ;
   We shall early meet again.

I'll remember thee, as morning
   Opes the gates of crystal day ;
I'll remember thee, as evening
   Sheds on earth its parting ray ;
I will love thee, trust, adore thee ;
   My heart's king, and prince of men !
God be with thee,—God protect us,—
   Kiss me, we shall meet again !

THE MEETING.

Two long years of cares and sorrows,
   Two great cycles wove above,
Two great links in our existence,—
   Have they been the links of love ?
I have struggled hard and conquered ;
   " For the sun shone in the sky " :

Do you love me now, my darling,
   As, when we did kiss Good-bye?

Dark has been the night of sorrow;
   Sweeter is the morn of joy.——
Glorious is the light of Phœbus,
   When it bursts day's canopy:
In the truthfulness of loving,
   In the constancy of life,
In the faithfulness of hoping,
   I have loved, to be your wife!

He who mounts the golden ladder,—
   She who weaves the silken thread,—
He shall bear her to the summit;
   She shall crown his weary head;
If each breast, to breast responsive,
   Blends two hopes in single faith,
Heaven seals life's loyal union,
   In life perfect after death.

A SONG.

WHISPER soft winds, where my true love lies sleeping;
   Softly, breathe softly, upon her sweet brow;
Tell her, her lover his vigil is keeping,
   Down by the stile, 'neath the whispering bough;
Softly, breathe softly, upon her sweet brow;
   Weave, in her dreams, the glad mem'ry of love;
Break not her slumbers; oh! gently blow,
   Bearing the fragrance of Eden above.

Scatter, bright stars, where my true love lies sleeping,
   Scatter thy hallowing rays on her breast;
Say her lone lover his vigil is keeping,
   Down in the bower that her fancy loves best,

Gently, shine gently, upon her sweet brow ;
  Breathe in her dreams the blest spirit of love ;
Break not her slumbers; oh ! gently glow,
  Bearing the radiance of heaven above.

TO M——.

In radiant joy, the purple sky
  All in the west is deeping;
And dappled clouds, like mottled shrouds,
  On silent forms, are sleeping ;
The fragrance of the evening breeze,
  On hill and vale is winging;
The drowsy murmurs of the bees
  In flowery groves are singing.

The light, that shines in crimson lines,
  I love to see it dally ;—
I love to see it leap and play
  On hill and purple valley.
But dearer still than golden hill,
  Or valleys softly darkling,
That witching light that trembles bright,
  From blue eyes sweetly sparkling.

SHE IS SLEEPING.

Spring is reigning, hearts are happy,
  Children laughing on the hill,
Blue-birds mating in the meadow,
  Wooing, warbling at their will ;
But my sorrow-shrouded bosom
Sings no song, admires no blossom :

>   She is sleeping, sleeping, sleeping,
>   Where the yellow willows wave;
>   She is sleeping, she is sleeping;
>   Love keeps vigil at her grave.

Nimble feet are sprightly dancing
  To th' ambrosial-blossomed grove;
Joy-lit eyes are sweetly glancing,
  Lips are kissing lips in love:
But my spirits only borrow
From their bliss the cup of sorrow:
  She is sleeping, sleeping, sleeping,
  Where the yellow willows wave;
  She is sleeping, she is sleeping;
  Love keeps vigil at her grave.

Joyous join in nature's anthem,
  Children, birds and zephyrs low;
Sparkle eyes, young hearts rejoicing
  Welcome Spring's reviving glow.
Let not my soul's secret anguish
Cause the chords of joy to languish;
  She is sleeping, sleeping, sleeping,
  Where the yellow willows wave;
  She is sleeping, she is sleeping,
  Love keeps vigil at her grave.

THE TRUANT-PLAYER'S SISTER.

ONCE in my life I taught a school
  As everybody knoweth,
And as this scraggy face of mine
  Most obviously sheweth;
Well, what I want to tell you is—
  The fact I know that *you* want—

That in my school I had a boy,
   A most inveterate truant.

Now, how it happened I can't tell,
   But yet 'tis true as preaching,
This urchin had a sister fair
   As Eve, and as beseeching;
And every time the little knave
   Struck out for a day's twister
Afraid to come to school next day,
   He'd kindly send his sister.

She'd stand in witching innocence
   And flatter most discreetly,
Until her little speech was done
   And I was gone completely;
For every time she deigned to smile
   In beauty that surpasses,
Up went my heart in a balloon
   Beyond the vain Parnassus.

She said her "ma" had confidence
   That I was true and noble,
But sent her down about *that boy*
   To tell me not to trouble.
Ha, ha, what cared I anyhow
   For him the ragged mister;
I'd have him truant every hour
   To see his pretty sister.

And so I let the truant youth
   Become a perfect Arab,
That I might drink the raptured smiles
   Of his sweet sister-cherub.
I guess he thought something was loose
   About the sharp resister;
The raw-hide and its champion too
   Were spoony on his sister.

When this began to stale, I said
  "My charming Miss McCarrol
Incorrigible he's become
  I'll have to use the ferule."
I kept the wicked notable
  In an eternal blister,
That I might get a thrashing from
  His wrathful, loving sister.

I made him howl, I made him dance,
  Dance juber, sing for freedom,
The stove-pipe climb, stand on his head,
  And every time I feed him.
And to appease the immortelle—
  I mean, you know, his sister—
I met her vengeance with a smile
  And then—well—then—I kissed her.

A jolly bachelor I am,
  As everybody knoweth,
And this indenture made this day
  Both witnesseth and sheweth;
But if I wished to wed—I don't—
  A trusty, leal assister,
I'd take St. Benedict's advice,
  And wed the truant's sister.

LIFE.

Step lightly! for an infant sleeps;
  His gambols close
  In blest repose;
Disturb him not; he sleeps!

Step lightly! for the warrior sleeps;
  The day is done;

The battle won ;
Disturb him not ; he sleeps !

Step lightly ! for the aged sleeps ;
There is no breath ;
He sleeps in death ;
Disturb him not ! he sleeps !

INCONSTANCY.

You say I am untrue, Mary ;
You declare I am untrue,
You vow I go acourting, Mary,
With other girls than you.

And so you are annoy'd Mary ;
I perceive you are annoy'd ;
You seem as though my art, Mary,
Had all your bliss destroy'd.

You will not let me see, Mary,
The sweet light of your eyes ;
You drown my little hope, Mary,
With tears, and sobs, and sighs.

Do you think I am a fool, Mary,
To court but half a maid ;
While others *all* in love, Mary,
Are waiting in the shade !

I treat maids, as they will, Mary ;
To truth, I'm constant, true ;
With flirts I am a flirt, Mary ;
To the proud, I'm pride, all through.

I know I'm rather poor, Mary,
   I'm poor in aught but love;
But my love can be as true, Mary,
   As the stars that shine above!

My cheek is wan and thin, Mary;
   And dim is my youthful eye;
My head hangs low;—Don't weep Mary—
   And my heart prays with a sigh.

Young George is lithe and light, Mary,
   For he burns no midnight oil;
Oh! happy his lot, indeed, Mary,
   For he never needs must toil.

As you've given him half your heart, Mary,
   You had better give him it all;
For *his* head is always *high*, Mary,
   He is gay, and young and tall.

It is hard to be light, erect, Mary,—
   It is hard to keep up the head,
When ascending the rough, steep hill, Mary,
   That the student's foot must tread.

When the form is buoyant, trim, Mary,—
   When the head is light and high,
'Tis because we are *going down*, Mary,
   Down the slope to misery.

Shake hands. No—no, good-bye! Mary!
   For, I could never bring
My lips to the lily hand, Mary,
   That wears another's ring.

And perhaps I may find *some* heart, Mary,
   To love me in days to come;—

I shall place my heart in hers, Mary,
  For an everlasting home!

The suns and the rolling spheres, Mary,
  May be sway'd from their destined course;
But my life shall be wound in hers, Mary
  While God rules the universe!

We have both this precept learnt, Mary,
  Let us treasure it preciously;—
That constancy of heart, Mary,
  Is bought with Constancy.

ON THE DEATH OF A FRIEND.

Grief's deadly pang has settled in my heart;
  I move in darkness of a starless night;
My soul, involved in clouds, will not depart
  From its dull deadness of relentless might.

A thousand voiceless sorrows' mingling tears,
  My budding hopes in their first impulse drown
There, in the sobbing floods of doubts and fears,
  There, there to perish have joy's nurslings flown.

Oh, for a song of woe to last for aye!
  Oh, for a flood that ne'er would cease to flow!
Friends and their friendship last but for a day—
  Falls the sweet flower, and pales its crimson glow!

Oh, Master Death! deceitful, heartless, cold,
  Thou universal despot of the earth!
All times and seasons thou art ever bold,
  From love and beauty to betray their worth.

A cycle short, in all life's giddy maze,
   The crown may reign upon the royal brow;
But, oh, that brow a *double* homage pays
   When to thy sceptre all its glories bow!

Few are the blessings human hearts enjoy—
   Few, when, alas! their constancy we weigh;
Friendship sincere, that earth cannot destroy,
   Our highest boast, and life's supreme display.

TO AN IDIOT CHILD.

God pity thee, my child!
   Rough enough, and hard the way
   Of life's tempestuous, vengeful sea,
For soul, for sight, for mind untried.

How vain for thee, poor dear,
   Smile the pearly orbs of heaven!
   How vain the bliss of day is given,
To make thy better cheer!

God pity thee! and send
   The light of glory on thy path;
   And guide thy darkened mind from wrath,
And save thee in the end!

Oh, reason, power divine!
   How sanctified and rapturous is life,
   When thou dost lead! Through hate and strife
Thy vigil star dost shine.

But, oh, how darkly sad,
   When contemplation of God's might
   Can never wake the soul from night.
The mind from 'mong the dead!

Th' immortal soul of man,
   God's earthly harp, lends no soft sound
   Melodiously sweet—no springs abound,
Till reason leads the van.

A mother's holy hand,
   With minist'ring love, thine own may press,
   May chafe those tiny feet, and dress
The glossy hair, in silken band,

In vain. In vain, fair blank,
   Is each caress and cheering word
   To thee, by rapture all unstirred,
No smile of childhood, playful prank.

Life in the vale of death!
   Action without thought—pain destitute of joy!
   Nor pleasing griefs, nor frisking hopes annoy!
Life without reason—only *breath!*

LOVE AND AUTUMN.

Purple, crimson, gold,
   Foreign fancy-queen,
Stands the stately wold
   Fading from the green.

Odors, like the breath
   Of oriental isle,
Slumbering beneath
   Fruit of summer toil.

Naked limbs arise
   From the grand array;

Piercing through the skies,
   In their mean dismay!

Slowly, slowly down,
   Like a warrior's blood,
Falls the faded crown,
   From the autumn wood.

Oh my heart is sad!
   For 'tis autumn there,—
All its zephyrs mad,
   All its forests bare.

For the summer sun,
   He, whose name is love,
Has my heart undone,—
   Took the wings of dove.

Death, and sin, and night,
   Children of despair,
Try unequal might
   For a heart, once fair.

If one form would die,
   If one image cease
Dwelling in my eye,
   All my hours were peace.

But, in rest or sleep,
   Whether sad or gay,
They that image keep—
   There *he* lives for aye!

Tall and slight and fair
   Graceful, goodly free;
Oh! my heart! how dare
   Bring him back to me!

I have said, " I hate "
    Darest thou admire ?
Is my earthly fate
    Wound in thy desire ?

Sing a song of woe
    All the autumn day ;
For my heart's my foe
    Stealing me away !

BEWARE !

BEWARE of him, who thinks, because
    His father is a millionaire,
He may infringe on Nature's laws
    And wave defiance to despair ;
For these are fancies light as air ;
Beware of him ! Beware ! Beware !

Beware of those who reckon toil,
    The symbol of a soiled heart,
And him who burns " the midnight oil,"
    The votary of deceitful art,—
Who say you are but what you wear ;
Beware of those ! Beware ! Beware !

Beware of him, a gilded moth
    Who floats about in indolence ;
Who, willing victim of his sloth,
    Becomes the slave of whim and sense ;
Who knows not how to do and dare,—
Beware of him ! Beware ! Beware !

Beware of him who deems success
The creature of a time or place ;

Who would not reck it idleness
To win the *phantom* of a race—
Be crowned with shadows of the fair,
Beware of him! Beware! Beware!

Who would be sculptor of a grace
   Yet dead, unchiselled from the block;
Who would not carve it from the maze,
   And rear it living from the rock—
Th' immortal monument of care;
Beware of him! Beware! Beware!

Beware of him whose heart but wins
   To boast a conquest made in vain;
Who counts it not among his sins
   To break a precious heart in twain,
Oh guard thy heart from him with care;
Beware of him! Beware! Beware!

Beware of that insiduous quaff,
   That burns the mind, that blinds the eye,
That makes its fool, a hero laugh
   Than laughs to see its victim die;
Oh, shun the most the *smiling* snare;
Beware my friend! My friend beware!

Beware of her who like a brave
   Strings triumphs on her chain of gold;
Who deems life long enough to waive
   A heart on which a heart lays hold—
Oh piteous life! Deluded fair!—
Beware of her! Beware! Beware!

GENIUS.

In half-unconscious, misty youth,
He heard the trembling voice of Truth
   Speak to his secret soul.
And strangely, wildly beat Life's flood :
Mysterious ecstacy of mood
   Did anger and condole.
Within the carnal cage, a bird
Its pinions plumed, its warblings stirred,
   And fluttered towards the goal.

In sleep he heard the mystic voice
Whose music made his soul rejoice,
   And gorified repose ;
It seemed, from the abyss of thought,
An under-current, wonder-fraught,
   That dyingly arose :
For purple-sailed the ships of gold,
Like the ephemeral kings of old,
   Rode on the billowy throes.

If but the lark's light matin-song,
He heard discoursing to the throng,
   It called to him, "*March On*";
While morning, radiant in her tears,
Inspiring hope, dispelling fears,
   Says unto him, "my son" ;
And every zephyr's gentle zest
Finds echo in his throbbing breast
   "There's Honor to be won"!

He heard the imperial myriarch's call
With trumpet-blast, his soul appal,
   In manhood's mighty hour ;
Till jubilant, with heavenly glow,
He raised his brow of flaming snow,

Responsive to its power:
The royal scion marched abroad
To do, to dare: Truth's golden rod,
   His sabre and his dower.

He saw purpureal splendor sleep
Upon the azure-bosomed deep,
   And zone the orient sky:
Renewed the voice,—the voice of Truth;
Flashed out the glorious flame of youth,
   Like lightning from his eye;
The hempen tablet glowed, instinct
With beauteous form and living, linked
   To matchless mystery.

Or warmed by Love's Platonic fire,
Or roused by Faith's soft thrilling lyre,
   Or tortured by Despair;
Or, when beneath the caustic wand
Of Sorrow's desecrating hand,
   Or in Remorse's lair;
How rude the hand that struck the chords
The truth of Truth,—the soul of words
   Stamped it the Poet's heir!

When, like soft wreathing cliffs of snow,
The locks of age o'erhung his brow,
   And dimness vailed his eye;
And, as the golden orb of life
Sank down within the vale of strife,—
   Sank slowly down to die;
In heaven, he heard the voice unsealed—
The voice of Genius,—Truth revealed
   In immortality!

YOUTH, LOVE AND THE GRAVE.

PALE, marble record of departed love,
   Forgive my lingering 'neath thy sacred shade;
Till I invoke the cherubim above
   To warble dirges of my senseless maid!

Here let me linger on this mound of clay,
   Embossed in green, and odorate with balm;
Here let me meditate, till ebbing day
   Shall cast her tears upon the holy calm.

O gentle love! so pure, so sweet, so young,
   To break my sorrow shalt thou ne'er return?
And must I leave my every charm unsung
   To wake the slumbers of thy silent urn?

Then I must muse in sorrow, and alone,
   O'er every joy we shared, in love and life:
No smile will cheer me, and no heart condone
   My erring portion, in the world's great strife.

The eye of affluence, the tongue of scorn,
   We recked unkind, but never insincere;
Our mutual care to meet at dewy morn,
   And part at evening, with a lover's tear!

How fair the rose-leaves on thy bosom bloom!
   And o'er thy brow, how soft the willows twine!
A tranquil glory hovers o'er thy tomb;
   Sweet is its breath, but sweeter far was thine!

The self-same songster, warbles on the spray,
   Whose mellow notes inspired our love of yore;
Oh, now awake! illume my weary way;
   And cheer me, with the song we loved, once more!

O love! arise; our woody path is strewn
    With gay, wild flowers in rude confusion sweet;
Oh! come; and let us wander forth, alone,
    And pluck the daisies, for thy bosom, meet.

As the dull shades of dusky, evening fall,
    I hear afar the hunter's echoing horn;
In woody dell, I hear the herd-bells call,
    And Philomel resumes his lay forlorn.

Then must young Spring her every charm display,
    The gladdening vale her every sweet disclose;
And thy poor lover sing his sweetest lay,
    In vain, to lure thee from thy long repose!

Then, be thy slumbers, as the sacred dead!
    Peace, joy and love, in holy union rise—
Immortal glory, o'er thy lowly bed;
    Thy soul, redeemed, await me in the skies.

Yet, not alone, shall thy sad lover stray,
    Though drops of grief shall tarnish every bliss:
For thy blue eye shall light along his way,
    And thy true bosom e'er repose in his.

The dark vicissitudes of varying time
    Oft darken portals eloquent with love:
But, reconciling man, in every clime
    We hear the mandates of a God above.

O may such blessed lot be ever mine,—
    My God to recognize in weal or woe!
O may my spirit ever dwell with thine,
    While I shall serve my pilgrimage below!

Blest be thy slumbers, as the sacred dead!
    Peace, joy and love, in holy union rise,—

Immortal glory crown thy lowly bed:
  Thy soul, redeemed, await me in the skies.

TO A——.

Can I ever forget thee, my darling?
  Can memory e'er prove untrue!
Shall misery, time or misfortune
  E'er cease me from thinking of you?

Thou art ever beside me, my darling;
  Thy image, all nature proclaims;
In sorrow it brings me enjoyment;
  In coldness my bosom inflames.

See the lights of the evening, my darling,
  All twinkling in innocent glee!
Then such is thy love to me darling,
  That beckons me ever to thee.

May thy blue eyes, in gladness, my darling,
  Ever smile 'neath the snow of thy brow;
May the hope that illumines thy bosom,
  Be constant and bright in its glow.

May the rosiest bowers of the morning,
  The grace of thy motion admire;
May the soft sighing zephyrs of evening,
  Fresh truth in thy bosom inspire.

I will never forget thee, my darling;
  Thou happiest gem of the earth!
Though I go,—and departing brings anguish—
  O, trust me! returning brings mirth.

MORN.

The peasant-song has woke the flowery dell;
   The eager mart has roused its matin bell;
And, on the cloudy mountain-brow, where night
   His lagging kingdom wheedles from the sight,
The cheerful shepherd, dewy as the morn,
   Fills the blue air with warblings of his horn;
Till voiceless zephyrs woo the rude refrain,
   And nature joins the universal strain.
The red-wing'd pilgrim, sedulously vain,
   Courts the dew'd rose, and wins her heart again;
His buzzing bumble, never in delay,
   In melancholy, lures the mind away;
Awake, thou sleeper! it is perfect day.

STEMMING THE STREAM.

Over the running stream,
   The engineer stood;
A darling boy, with a violet eye,
   Serious in his mood.

His high brow, soft and white,
   By raven tendrils clasp'd;
One outstretched hand was his only wand,
   The other a willow grasp'd.

Trying to stem the stream,
   His mind was troubled deep
Though a very child; but his fancy smiled
   At the scheme in its golden keep.

Trying to stem the stream,
   With sands, and straws, and wood,

His young heart wept, as he saw them swept,
  Adown in the laughing flood.

Trying to stem the stream;
  A tear bedew'd his eye,
He ventured the wave, and he found a grave
  Where the wave-washed pebbles lie!

Oh! what a picture, this,
  Of man's ambitious soul;
Forgetting all for the siren call
  Of fame at her laurelled roll!

Trying to stem Fate's stream,
  With hopes, and tears, and faith,
Urging his soul to a shadowy goal
  He drifts on the tide of death!

CANADA'S SONS TO THEIR SIRES.

Toll the bell, and toll it slowly; let the echoes mournful rise:
Sound the dead march of the battle, while the swelling requiem dies!
From the homes so fondly cherished, from the dear ones, fair and bright;
From the scenes and recollections, that have filled them with delight;
Lo! our fathers, martyrs, heroes, daily passing from our view,
From the world of false and fleeting, to the realms of bright and true.

From the deep unbroken forest, they have hewn our happy homes;
From the giants of the forests, they have reared our glittering domes.

Still we see the axe uplifted; still we hear the woodland ring;
See the thundering hemlocks falling prostrate to their sturdy king:
Still we hear their native chorus ling'ring, dying in the grove;
See the sickles strongly wielded; see the brawny muscles move.

As we ponder to contemplate all their nobleness of soul,
Daring courage, pious patience, honest reason and control;
When we think them persevering, sacrificing all for us,
Toiling, battling, hoping, praying; how in gratitude we bless!
How we wonder if we ever shall accomplish deeds so grand,
If our loyalty and valor will protect our fathers' land.

Noble was their cause and country; nobly was their cause maintained;
They have bravely fought and conquered; and immortal glory gained.
For, upon broad History's pages, there's no record more sublime,—
Art and Science have no patrons worthier on their book of time—
Than the genial independence, social joy, and love sincere,
Strength of courage, faith and reason, that our fathers held so dear!

On the earth, no calling higher, than the hand that holds the plough;
Not the soldier's palm of triumph; not the poet's laurelled brow.
Genius may enroll her children, on the golden scroll of fame;
But the monument of glory, Industry must ever claim,

Onward ! onward ! ever onward, speed the cause of honest
    worth :
May the stainèd hand of labor, honored be, while rolls the
    earth.

They have left, with all its grandeur, Caledonia's heathered
    hills,
Land of scholars, nurse of poets, where the shepherd's
    pibroch thrills.
They have left the gentle valleys, flowing hills, and rip-
    pling streams,
That make England's mild expanses earnest of unending
    dreams.
They have left the land of beauty, isle of warmth and wit
    and worth,
Clime of eloquence and passion, home of chivalry and
    mirth !

Chose the music of the forest for the murmur of the wave ;
Left on shore their friends forsaken, dear ones sleeping in
    the grave ;
Chained their beauty and their laughter, in the bondage
    of their strength ;
Fought with hardships, dangers, trials ; conquered all, and
    won, at length.
Where the blue smoke of their shanties curled above the
    western wood,
There the smiling fields and pastures bask in evening's
    purple flood.

They are going, ever going ; but their mem'ry, beaming
    bright,
Will reanimate our bosoms, actuating to the right ;
We, by honor, shall endeavor, with strong ever-grateful
    hearts,
To be brave in every battle ; in each scene, to take our
    parts ;

For their noble blood is in us, and their patriot spirit
    high ;
They have won for *us* and perished, we shall fight for
    them, or die.
Toll the bell, and toll it slowly ; let its throbbings softly
    rise :
Sweetly, sadly, keep it ringing, at each knell a hero dies !

A LESSON.

SILENTLY through boundless space,
    Moves the mighty train of spheres ;
Speeding in the mystic chase ;
    Rolling cycles to the years.
They revolve imperiously,—
    Yet silently—so silently.

Softly down the stilly air
    Falls the snow-flake, crystalled, white,
Robing fields and forests bare
    In the garments of delight ;
Then resumes its home on high,·
    Yet silently—so silently.

Silently the orb of day
    Rises high, anon reclines.
Silently, all night's array
    Holds its vigil as it shines.
Time's chariots roll all gloriously,
    Yet silently—so silently.

Silently, the power of faith,
    Hope and constancy and love,
Lead across the vale of death,
    To the throne of light above :

God rules the world mysteriously,—
   Yet silently—so silently.

Silently, the human mind,
   Busy with the busy heart,
Rears of thought a world combined,
   Culls from chaos, system, art;
Bringing light from mystery,—
   Yet silently—so silently.

TO AN OLD MAID.

ALAS! a beautiful lily,
   Blooming in perfect Spring-day,
Caught in November air chilly,
   Petals all shrivelled and gray.
When Beauty's mature,
Make harvest-day sure.

Alas! a fancy-winged warbler,
   Charming with eloquent song,
Neglecting to act as the garbler
   Of Gold from the Brass of the throng;
Lingering late in the woe
Of Autumn's unmerciful snow.

Oh, would you live wisely fair lady?
   Marry, young maiden, when fair;
Beauty, like summer, grows shady,
   Seared by intemperate air;
Be mindful fair lady of duty;
For swift is the wing of your beauty.

FOR A LITTLE GIRL'S ALBUM.

"Maiden with the meek brown eyes,
In whose orbs a shadow lies,"
May the light, that, lingering there,
Shines upon thy features fair,
Live within and lead thee on,
Upward, upward to the throne,—
Never leave that happy home,
Through the changeful hours that come ;
Never may its guardian ray
Fly on eager wings away.

Long, upon thy beauteous brow,
Live the love that graces now ;
May youth's holy innocence
Stay, and be thy heart's defence;
Sweetly, may thy rosy lip,
From the cup of wisdom, sip ;
Lightly may thy bosom bear
All its human lot of care ;
Ever may glad Beauty seek
Refuge on thy lily cheek ;
And, when life's bright star shall sink
Dead behind the mystic brink,
To a glorious paradise,
May thy soul in transport rise.

LINES SUGGESTED BY THE DEATH OF WILLIAM CULLEN BRYANT.

      Ambitious youth!
Behold yon golden king his vestal course
Assume, and mount up to his orient throne.
Mark, as he mounts, how spreads his lucid plume,
His brow becomes a cresset of rich light,
Diffusing to the far off realms of sky
Its wakeful ray, until the vasty dome
Becomes a temple of celestial cheer,—
E'en prosy clouds their borders prinking white—
Appearing as quaint dowagers dusk-brow'd—
From isles remote, in coronets of pearl.
Observe, as sinks his golden trail, at eve,
What copious halos deepen on the face
Of fading day,—what thronging galaxy
Of constellated orbs, lights heaven's arch—
All imitating and diffusing light—
Their legacy from the supremer king.
Such is the ebb and flow of mortal power;
Thus, frequent as that period call'd day
Revolves its splendors o'er the gladdened earth
Thou hast an emblem of our lot.

        So rose
Immortal Bryant, panting for the crown;
His boyish zeal, at first, with eager eyes
Perusing long-hid lore, from library,
Still fountful in its ancient fire; anon
Blushing beneath the punishment of praise,
Deserved and honest, from some critic won;
Till, bursting fulgent, like the star of morn,
Proclaiming by one noble daring leap,
The genius and the valor of his soul,
Despising rude restraint from bootless bore,

Plunging, all fearless, o'er the curling waves
Of jealous scorn, of envious critic's pride;
And, recking all unworthy of his thoughts,
The red-eyed passions of the madding throng,
His mind, thus, he in constancy maintained;
Until, in high meridian majesty,
Its warmth and light inestimable shed
O'er the wide earth, casting a splendor on
The meanest thing, that such exalteth to
The noble dignity of thought; lending
Wisdom, glory, eloquence and joy unto
The universal brotherhood of dust!
And, when this spirit, gloriously had
Reared, from inception quite oblivious,
The sovereign passion of his soul; and won
Its lot a consummation so divine;
That it, like Alcyone, might e'ermore,
Shine forth and revel in its ecstacy,—
Then,—when the task was throughly beautified,
Then,—as effulgent splendor clothed each scene,
Then,—sank the sun; and, as it faded dim,
O! didst' thou not behold, how cycles bright
Of faith and love wove in the essence red
Of waning life! O! didst thou not behold,
While on the altar's sacrificial floor,
The great devoted life was consecrated,
What incense filled the air; ascended then
To heaven; and, what a choir seraphic rose,
Attuned their notes to sweet harmonious parts,
That blended in melodious concord soft;
Until each soul of earth arose; and pale
And languid, with his vigil set atrim,
Whispered "farewell!"

      When dies the wit, savant,
Philosopher, a meagre school laments
The sad decease; for such are apt to be

Too apathetic to that subtle thread
Of faith that holds man obligate to man;
But, when the poet quits his earthly bower,
Wide as the world, the stream of sorrow flows,
Nor are such mournings the idle impulse
Of passing dreams; but righteous tribute
T' exalted worth. The true-born poet is
The nation's noblest gift. His theme unites
Mercy, Justice, Peace, Love, and best of all,
That star that beacons with its gentle film,
The fainting sp'rit to portals bright above.
His avocation is the voice of life ;
To thoughts divine, his aspiration leads.
In every walk, his mind is most supreme ;
Most liberal and wise his tenets are ;
His pen the happiest instrument of state.

Its sway illumes and dignifies the world ;
'Tis all abounding as the balmy air ;
It steals invisibly through all our lives,
Being present always as essential good,
Nor scorns it poverty, nor fawns on wealth,
It stems the boastful arrogance of power,
By whisp'ring to the rich that they are poor,
And pointing to the world imperishable.
Lo ! what a world of blest content it brings
Unto the lowly poor, whose hope on earth
Is weary toil. It leads them by the hand ;
In mellow tones breathes, " Blessed are the poor ; "
Till every grief becomes a hallowed pang ;
The scalding sweat of toil a promise fair
Of bliss beyond the grave ; and mis'ry's crust
Becomes a bounteous feast of life-fraught food,
And, the hard pillow, softer than the crown
Of throned king. It chides the simple soul ;
Incites the wise ; speaks wisdom to the young ;
And makes the tepid blood of age course on

With manly force, in animated pride;
Till, the old heart steals bravely back to youth,
Forgetful of the crown of snow. On each
Green isle, hid in the expanse of the sea,
It breathes; in every clime, its sympathy
Is felt through seasons in their annual roll;
Makes winter kind; spring, glad; and summer, cool;
And autumn, a sweet dream of fading flowers.
It gives to thought its mingling light and shade,
'Tis like a glorious, calmly flowing stream,
That, with a placid surf and depth unknown,
In stately silence, sweeps along its course,
In cortex bright of an eternal spring.
'Midst tranquil bliss its fragrant banks repose.
Embosomed in bright solitude, we hear
The rustling leaves play with the dallying breeze.
There, wild and foreign song-birds, clad in gold,
On glittered wing flit through the bower, their throats
All quivering to the eloquence of joy.
There, we may sit with nature's humble rose;
There, snatch our destiny from every wave;
And, meditating there in splendid peace,
We hear naught but instruction's lowly voice;
And see in every dewdrop, on the rose,
The image of omniscient God!
                                         Yes, such
Distinguished attributes, our sister-land
Is mourning, as embodied in her bard!
What though they rear the epitaphic rock
To stand the emblem of a nation's grief,
A sorrowing nation's gratitude to bear!
Those signs shall undecipherable grow;
With all their splendor crumble in decay,
And those who graved them deep, as monster Time
Shall wheel his headlong chariot o'er them all,
Yet though such rude vicissitudes uprise,
The writing of glad memory's hand to mar;

When, o'er the ashes of departed worth,
New generations shall awake to fame,
In brave defiance to relentless Time,
They shall behold in deathless lustre still,
That *everlasting* monument—his work,—
Increasing in its pride and brilliancy ;
While flowing soft, to every land and tongue,
The treasured name of BRYANT shall remain
A sacred word, a household gift and charm !
Thus shall the words and thoughts of wise and good
Mementos be forever of themselves,
And rule with Time, till he shall be unthroned.

THY BROTHER.

SLOW-PACED, and tottering with age, and feeble with decay,
His languid eyes are wet and dim, his long loose tresses, gray,
He comes the trembling wreck of fate, the palsied child of woe,
To ask the homage of your heart, and shelter from the snow.
O speak to him in kindly deed ; nor send him to another ;
Remember ; thou thyself art man ; remember, he's thy brother !

THE SEA BY MOONLIGHT.

THE soft waves are dashing and foaming and splashing,
  Down by the beautiful shore !
Now gracefully gliding, their passion subsiding,
  They sink as the murmurs of yore.
The dull shadows lending, to green hills ascending,
  The fleet, veering, magical mood ;

While dark rocks uprearing, like giants appearing,
   Arise from the musical flood.

The blue, alpine grandeur, arrayed in dark splendor,
   Just looming afar, wakes the soul;
The sea's broken whispers, the night-birds' shrill vespers
   Give song to the waves as they roll.
Now charging, recoiling, in white foam aboiling,
   Breasting the rocks on the shore,
Their deep iry breathing, in white spray-clouds wreathing,
   Like white manèd chargers of war!

O, spirit of the ocean! how great thy devotion,
   To rock in the arms of the deep;
And, far down, to slumber, where green waves encumber
   The tranquillity of thy sleep!
O love! be not frightful; the scene is delightful;
   Music and beauty in ire!
Such wooing and wailing, such laughter and railing!
   Such minglings of pathos and fire!

LOVE'S OFFERING—A FLOWER.

PLUCKED from thy virgin stem, sweet flower,
   In tender bloom,
Dost thou, fair form, not weep? Forgive the power,
   Forget thy doom!

For if thou could'st but know the joy
   Thou bring'st to me;
Methinks thy little bosom would ally
   In ecstacy.

Those slender fingers plucking thee in haste,
   Plucked thee in love

And preference; to show, that in her breast,
   Thy essence wove.

Thou star of hope, thy sweetly fragrant breath,
   Thy roseate hue,
Remember me of love that knows no death,—
   Love ever true.

And in thy spotless, crimson, dewy garb
   The virtue pure
That, when dark grief my feelings did disturb,
   Was silent cure.

Yes! bright epitome, for ever in thy face
   I see her form,
Her virtue, beauty, constancy and grace,
   Her heart so warm!

Oh! I shall ne'er forget thee, dearest heart,
   Thy image bright
Shall cheer my wanderings though we're far apart,
   My pathway light.

For I shall wreathe this emblem on my lyre,
   As laurel spray;
It shall, to song, arouse my latent fire,
   To think of thee.

Its bloom may wither, and its beauty fade,
   Its form decay;
Yet I'll preserve it, ever, dearest maid,
   Thy truth to me.

And, when, no more, the poet's faltering muse
   Shall cherished be,—
When fate forbids what trembling love would choose,
   A smile from thee;

Then, on this sweet memento will I gaze,
　　With dewy eye;
And, in reflection, count the happy days
　　Long, long gone bye!

And dream of youth, by rude experience taught
　　To love in vain,
And hope by merit to obtain my lot,
　　'Gainst lust of gain.

THE SOLDIER BOY.

The vestal stars were paling
　　In the pearly glow of morn,
When the young and dauntless soldier
　　Was roused by the battle-horn.
When, riding his noble charger,
　　To join in the battle-cry,
He drew his rein and dismounted
　　To bid his love good-bye.

A touch of lips, hands pressing,
　　And a hurried, sad "good-bye,"
Then the fair young maid stood praying
　　For her valiant soldier-boy.
They marched away to glory,
　　To fight for their native land;
In all that host, not a faltering heart,
　　Not a weak or unwilling hand.

The thunder of the battle
　　Broke the stillness of the night,
When the daring sons of freedom
　　Charged the legions of the night;

And, brave amongst the bravest,
   Was our hero. Though so young,
His heart was true, his soul was brave,
   His arm was great and strong.

His comrades fell around him,
   But he paused to shed no tear;
'Twas his to fight and conquer,
   So he rushed on with a cheer.
They won, and when the battle o'er,
   They homeward marched again,
No braver heart nor sadder brow
   Did weep the noble slain.

But, when he met the maiden
   To find her prove untrue,
His heart, the bravest of the brave,
   Beat once, and burst in two;
Thus he, dying, said:—"My comrades
   I fight for victory—
I march away to glory,
   I conquer or I die."

THE LOST HOPE.

BELOVED thou art gone! My eyes have ceased
Their sorrowing; but burns, still deep within
My heart and mind the hidden flame of hope
That lit, can ne'er—sad truth—be quenched. A hope
Departing is a tardy boat, that leaves
You watching on the shore, and bears itself
Away; its path so gentle and direct,
You cannot see its motion, and, at times,
You deem it nearing; but alas it aye
Recedes away, away, away, until

It melts into the purple azure of
The border-line; and you are pensive, mute
Upon the strand, with tear-moist eye, and in
Your heart a yearning, voiceless something sad
Whose dull eternal pain you cannot quench;
Nor what, nor why it is, can you define.

Is hope a rude misnomer, a deceitful thing,
That leads but to destroy, wins to betray;
Or is it but the earthly counterpart
Of a sublimer star, that dwells away
In some Elysian abode, to which
The earthly tries to lead? Thus must it be:
Then, haply, one sad day, the vail shall rend;
Effulgent light shall burst; the faithful meet;
And hopes long lost on earth, but ne'er forgot,
Shall shine resplendent in our crown of peace!

THOMAS CARLYLE.

In Memoriam.

The sun has set; but, ling'ring in the sky,
Kissing its stainless azured canopy,
The purple west is shot with golden lines.
While evening in her burnished couch reclines,
Her gorgeous children, in her portals, play;
And crimson porters close the gates of day.
The weary world, enchanted by the charms,
Across its bosom folds its myriad arms;
And, half-beguiled by the sublime array,
The roseate essence, aftermath of day,
Forgets the bursting, billowy flood unblest,
That, palpitating, swells its aching breast;

Till, unforbidden, from th' abyss of thought,
The deep soul-language, mystic, heaven-fraught,
Strains, like Prometheus from his cursèd chains;
Swells, like the ocean sweeping o'er the plains.
Each throbbing echo beats one sacred word;
Attunes the universe one rapturous chord;
Uprising incantations heaven-inspired,—
The apotheoses of hearts deep fired,—
Beat at the pearly gates of paradise,
Bearing the fragrance of a nation's voice.

From every clime, where Learning's page unfolds;
Or Truth, o'er Ignorance, her sceptre holds;
Solemn and low, the sorrow-tributes swell,—
Great, good Carlyle, the friend of Truth, farewell!

Thy sun has set. Yet, from thy fettered tomb
Truth's radiance dissipates the ebon gloom;
For though thy honor'd ashes sleep in peace,
Thy flame of genius ever shall increase.
From the bright laurel, that thy brow entwines,
The splendid effluence of glory shines;
And, from that shrine where reverent nations mourn,
Breathes the supernal fulgence of the morn.
Fresh from the crystal fountain of thy soul,
With ceaseless tide, the streams of wisdom roll;
While love humane, and tenderness combined,
Sheds lustre on the grandeur of thy mind.
When the dread clouds of ignorance and vice
Spread their eclipsing pinions o'er Truth's eyes,
How strong thy arm, how sharp thy sword to smite,
And usher in the matchless realms of Light!

In youth's delightful hour, when sweet delay
Allures the languid world with transient ray,
Untrue to youthful joy, and selfish aim,
Thou panted at the golden gate of Fame;

Thou, with the vigil reigning on thy brow,
Sought the deep mines, unnumbered fathoms low;
Where, in the dark environments of night,
The pearls of Truth lay hidden from all sight,—
All save that penetrating glance of thine,
That seemed to flash the light of the divine.
Here coulds't thou pierce, with heav'n illumined gaze,
The secret wonders of the mystic maze,—
Here could'st thou snatch, from shadow-loving death,
The star of morning and the prophet's breath,—
Thy subtle mind found sweet instruction here,
And gracious thoughts a sorrowing world to cheer.
At day's meridian, black with sweat and soil,
O'er-freighted with the precious fruit of toil,
In conflict weary, yet, in valor strong,
Mighty in right, and spurning every wrong,
Wise in thy purpose, didst thou hold thy path,
Despite vain critics in affected wrath.
Thy faithful labors to conclude with day,
The ev'ning found thee, with its parting ray,
Sowing thy toil-begotten pearls abroad,
To rise from earth and blossom up to God,
Then, when thy long, long day of earth did close,
Thrice weary heart, thou laid thee at repose.

Sleep! Sleep! Thou glorious lion-warrior sleep.
Truth, like an angel, shall her vigil keep
Above that hallow'd spot, that boasts thy clay,
Lighting mankind its doleful debt to pay.
The task shall each essay with falt'ring soul—
To weave a dirge above the hero's goal;
In the pale marble of the deathless dead,
To carve a niche above the glorious head;
To mark whereon the quenchless orb of day,
In earth's oblivion, dimmed its beacon ray;
And, sighing, drop a consecrating tear
Upon the laurels of th' immortal seer,

There shall the poet, thinking of thy fame,
Strike his dull lyre and wake its smould'ring flame.
There, too, the warrior of the coming age
Shall fan the ardor of his righteous rage.
To gild the fabric of his fancy's might,
The painter there shall snatch the threads of light.

Rest worshipp'd ashes! Rest immortal dead!
Millions are weeping o'er th' insensate head,—
Millions, in bounty of thy festal page,
'Midst wondering grief, their tears in truth assuage!

Man of few books and eagle-pinion'd thought,
Above all canons by wise critics taught;
Thy great book, Nature; and thy mind thy rule;
All schools despising; master of a school;
No stinted numbers, aptly polished phrase,
To please the wrong, and half the right to praise,
Came from thy soul with half-intentioned might;
Thy soul sat still or took a lofty flight.
When, to a cause thy eloquence was given,
It was the rolling thunder-car of heaven,
By tempest-steeds propell'd, in awful ire,
Cleaving the trembling clouds with track of fire.
And, like a massive avalanche that slides,
With wasting crash down alpine mountain-sides,
Thus down on superstitions' cherish'd spot,
Swept the strong torrent of thy burning thought,
As he of old who smote Mount Horeb's side;
And bade the issues from its fountains glide;
So on thy power the thirsting myriads gazed;
And drank its potions, whilst they stood amazed.
As, at the wak'ning touch of fancy's wings,
The image, living from the marble springs;
So when thy genius soared in heavenward flight,
Truth sprang exultant from the grasp of night;
Love, mantling in protection of thy might,
Made no display, but smiled in calm delight.

True Philomath ! Thou took not science fair,
To place her shining robes on black despair,—
Styling an uncreated Science, God.
To thee, she beckoned with her golden rod,
Enthroned in greatness, to a greater still,
Divine in wisdom, and supreme in will.
Thy Law, the universe-combining cord,
That moves obedient to the regnant word;
Thy art, the emblem of the unseen hand,
Stamp'd on the mind, and making nature grand.
No kindred mind shall ope thy golden page,
But trust and love shall doubt and fear assuage;
Nor search the mystic mirror of thy mind,
But God reflected in its depths shall find!

Warm-hearted friend to struggling, suff'ring youth,
Crazed with insatiable lust for Truth.
Through all the gilded mockery of lore,
Vainly he battles for the looming shore;
Scorn'd by the rude, and to the great unknown,
He stems the tide, or sinking, dies alone,
How few, the arms that stretch above the wave,
Careful the wrecking mariner to save !
But thou, upon the eminence of Fame,
And, in immortal light embalmed, thy name,
Though Captain of the jewell'd fleet of state,
Could succor those who falter'd with their fate;
And chart the bearings with a pilot's hand,
Solicitous that Right should reach the land.

Thy part of earth's afflictions hadst thou, too,—
Without a hope, to toil, long battles through;
Or, if a hope illumed thy starless path,
To see it shatter'd at the shrine of wrath;
To win the help, the love, the faith, the heart,
To warm, to praise, to light thy wondrous art;
And, then alas ! ere ev'ning's mellow light
Had touch'd that bosom with its essence bright;

To lay the hand of help, the heart of worth,
Forever silent in the slumbrous earth,
But upward to its source, that soul aspired
On angel wings, in robes of love attired ;
As though a rose should blow, a star above,
To win its votary to holier love,
There, wrapt in light resplendent, sanctified,
Eternal marriage shall restore thy bride ;
There Scotia's bard, the erring child of love,
Shall meet and welcome thee to fame above.

High Priest of letterdom ! Imperial soul !
Prince of pilosophers ! Upon the roll
Of glory, bright, illustrious, deathless star,
That not the din of earth may move nor mar !
Above thee, shall a reverend nation's voice
Rear the pale record of its sovereign joys ;
And grave in fadeless characters thy name,
Enshrouded by the nimbus-crown of fame.
But Time's all desecrating hoof may stamp
The marbled book to earth. The vestal-lamp
Earth-kindled, at the threshold of thy tomb
Shall pale its ray in night's oblivious gloom ;
But Time's loud tempest shall thy flame relume,
And make eternal from the shadowing doom ;
While centuries shall bring thy prophecies
Within the vision-bound of other eyes ;
Far age succeeding age new grandeur find
In the vast Pantheon of thy kingly mind ;
And long as earth love Might, Truth, Liberty,
Children shall lisp and nations boast of thee !

NATURE'S ECHOES.

ALL around are dying echoes
    From the golden harps unseen;
Songs unheard, in softest cadence,
    Ever fading, ever green.
Like the swell of heavenly music,
    Falling snow-soft down the air,
Come the raptured notes of nature,
    From her myriad muses fair.

Deep'ning shadows linger round us,
    Melancholy, yet sublime;
Wrapt in solitude their glory;
    Silence is their magic rhyme.
Whither come they? Ah, we know not,—
    Down the long, long age of time,
They are borne as nature's phantoms
    Echoes from her minster chime.

Years have rolled and left their shadows;
    Friends have gone, yet lives their faith;
Hopes have died nor yet departed;
    Nothing dies at death but death.
Soft, low songs, so sweet and solemn,
    Sung by those we loved of yore,
Live forever in our mem'ry
    Echoes from the other shore.

Pregnant with supernal grandeur,
    Pathos, beauty, sorrow, rage
Is each whisper of Æolus
    To inspire us, and assuage.
Twilight has its mystic language;
    Darkness sings its silent song;
Morning's lips of dewy roses
    Speak in kisses to the throng.

Words and deeds of wise and noble
   Grow in brilliancy and worth;
While the stars and rocks and forests,
   Hold the beauty of their birth;
For the patient, toiling poet
   Speaks but to the ear; while roll
Nature's symphonies sublimer
   In the language of the soul.

Whispers soften, loud words anger;
   More convincing to the wrong
Is the eloquence of silence,
   Than the kindlings of the tongue,
Thus we love the light and wisdom,
   Flung like shadows of the past;—
These are echoes of the glory,
   We shall comprehend at last.

THE DAUGHTERS OF THE WEST.

(A Song.)

You may sing from morn till evening,
   On your silvery laurelled lyre;
And invoke the gods of music
   With your genius all afire,—
You may sing of foreign beauty
   Till you burst your aching breast;
But *I'll* sing from morn till evening,
   Of the daughters of the West.

On the barren hills of Northland,
   You have seen the charming fair,
With her sweet and smiling manners,
   And her wealth of golden hair;

And you thought if you could win her
    There could be *one* mortal blest;
But sweeter far, and comely
    Are the daughters of the West.

You have met her in the Rhineland,
    With her ruby lips of love,
Her eyes like lakes all sunlit,
    And her gracefulness amove;
In the palm-groves of Italia,
    In the vineyards of old France,
On the purple-crowned Lusania,
    You have seen them laugh and dance.

There was rapture in their bosoms;
    Their was music in their hearts;
While their dark, soft, dreamy eyeballs
    Spoke a word that ne'er departs;
Till a melancholy madness
    Caussed your heart to feel oppressed;
But rein your heart; until you see
    The daughters of the West!

On the shores of clear Geneva,
    You have seen the beauteous Swiss
Making hay to sweetest music,
    Making home a scene of bliss;
On her head a homely Tuscan,
    And a garland round her waist;
Yet even *they* are shadows of
    The daughters of the West!

SORROW.

Tenderly! tenderly! lay her to rest,
    Down in the cold damp earth;
Place the sweet lily of peace on her breast,
    Emblem of beauty and worth.

Beautiful! beautiful! slumber in peace!
    Vain are the toil and strife
Of this wheeling world, and its jostling race
    To rouse from thy better life.

As a fading flower, as a golden hour,
    Passes the time of youth;
Like a hidden gem in a deep sea-bower,
    Life is a mystic truth!

Mournfully! mournfully! lay her to sleep,
    Dark in the shades of death;
Mournfully turn from the bier to weep,—
    Sigh with a parting breath!

Hopes that have cheered, joys that have smiled,
    Wither and die in their bloom;
A heart that beat warm, and the truth of a child,
    Sink in the merciless tomb!

Yet will come a day, now fleet on the way,
    To chill our heart with its breath;
Beauty and love, wealth, honor's array
    Seek but the slumber of death.

Now we depart; but, from the heart,
    Absence can never unlink;
The long chain of love still reaches above,
    And carries us over the brink!

A THOUGHT.

How like a dream is life! It hath its sleep;
   It is a thing unreal in a way;
Estival haloes, coralline and deep,
   In pristine cortege, purl our halcyon day;
But Hope's coronal, bright as it may be
   Can only prink Existence' billowy bank,
In cortex brighter than the gloomy sea;
   While toiling multitudes, whose craft have sank,
The sea's deceptive rocks, and waves of angry pride
   Are all forgot, while gazing, struggling for the margin's
      side!

TO A KIND FRIEND.

SET Life's little rose
   In a garden fair;
There alone it blows,
   Sheds its perfumes there;

For the heart most warm,
   Soon must chill in death,
When Life's wintry storm
   Freezes every breath.

Dearest hopes of earth
   Perish in a day,
If their tender birth
   Meets no kindred ray.

Oh how many hearts
   Perish every hour,
Struggling with parts
   Greater than their power!

TO A KIND FRIEND.

Help the palsied hands;
   Comfort hearts who mourn;
Quickly run Life's sands,
   Never to return.

There's a golden crown,
   If a crown be given;
There's a record down,
   In the books of heaven;

Not for idle wealth,
   Not for kingly bearing,
Not for healing health,
   Not for needless daring;

But for him whose mind
   Thinks of those in sorrow;
Thinks of all his kind
   Shuddering for to-morrow!

Oh, what broken hearts!
   Oh, what failing lives!
Oh, what cruel darts!
   Oh, what heavy gyves!

Can a smile relieve,
   Can a word revive,
Can a hope retrieve,
   Can a kiss outlive!

Long as Life will last;
   Long as hearts adore;
Long as Love holds fast
   To its ancient lore;

In my life, a gem;
   In my heart, a shrine;

In my love, a dream ;
   Shall be ever thine !

Since thy sunny smile
   Cheered my lonely heart ;
Through life's little while,
   Thou shalt ne'er depart.

LOST.

A GLORIOUS dream was in my brain,
   When a sudden shock
   My slumbers broke ;
And I never could splice my dream again.

A glowing thought came from my heart ;
   But I had no page
   For the treasure sage,
And fleet as a swallow it did depart.

I loved a maiden beauteous, dear ;
   I turned to wait
   For the prompt of fate ;
I lost the prize, though I was sincere.

I found a line of wisdom, grace ;
   But I turned away
   Till some other day ;
And I never again could find the place.

O, many a golden-freighted life,
   By a swaying breeze,
   From its troubled peace,
Is lost in the waves of hungry strife !

O, many a precious soul thus dies,
  Turning the eye,
  To say good-bye,
To some fascinating lust or vice!

MARRIAGE HYMN.

Oh, sweetly the billows are sleeping!
  From the rosy, the radiant shore,
We have pushed our boat; we are keeping
  Our course for the Evermore.
Lightly may the breakers play;
Love our star, and Hope our way
  We shall reach the Evermore!

Oh, brightly the heavens are beaming:
  While our sails are zephyr-blown,
Our Love's fair craft is dreaming
  To the pale of the sweet Unknown.
Halcyon may the blue profound
Ever slumber! Onward-bound,
  We shall reach the sweet Unknown!

But how shall we fare when the ocean
  Shall leap in tempestuous glee?
We shall toil, love, hope in devotion,
  For the port of the Deathless Day.
From the angry, seething flood,
Casting faithful eyes to God,
  We shall reach the Deathless Day!

A morn, thus blest, on her dewy wings,
   Had risen to perfect, glorious day,
When the trembling form of a gray old man
   Slowly advanced on his tottering way.
His step, half-stay'd by the grasp of time—
   His slight form bent by the weight of years;
But a spirit of Faith and Love divine
   Shone up to heaven through his hoary hairs.
He was all alone! on his lingering path,
   No arm supported his faltering frame;
And he looked like a pilgrim far from his home,
   Yet led by the light of its quivering flame.

And, there, as he gazed, on either hand,
   The red hills rose to the azure sky;
And the strange, wild thrill of reviving youth
   In his bosom throbb'd, and danced in his eye.
But it quickly died, for the winter's snow
   Would soon be a shroud for the earth's warm breast;
He sighed: for *his* winter came long ago,
   And he only awaited the spring-day rest.

By his calmly mien, and his meek, white brow,
   And the firm composure of cheek and eye,
You might readily guess his labor of life—
   Yes, he taught in the cottage of logs near by.
In that cottage of logs, with its quaint brown door,
   With its rustic roof, and its crumbling walls,
While the earth went round in her mystic dance,
   For two score times in the world's great halls,
He had seen green spring, when Auster's breath
   Had roused in her bosom the hope of joy;
He had seen when the merciless wind of death
   Had robbed the rose of its daintiest dye;
In pains, in sorrows, in coldness, in fear,
   He had suffered, and waited, and wept, and prayed.

A TRIBUTE.

Fair is thy brow, thy cheek most beautiful;
Thy lips seem fashioned for a rosy kiss;
Thy eyes are like the liquid moon,
When dropping full of pearly essence
From the archway of an ebon cloud;
The perfect art of Nature is thy chin.
As when the ocean moon-lit, white,
Heaves with a gentle sigh its rounded wave,
Unbroken, mirroring the sky,
So swells the spirit in thy breast
Moving the surface lily-white.
With soft entwinings of its tendril curls
Down thy slight form, comes
All the floating grandness of thy hair:
It kisses, with its lucid lip, thy cheek;
And vailing half thy lovely breast,
With half its sableness of hue,
Makes still more lovely that is beautiful.

But 'tis not eye, nor cheek, nor lip,
That I adore, 'tis something grander,—
Something, from thine eye, that shines,—
Something, that smiles around thy lip,—
Something that leaves its crimson
Foot-marks on thy cheeks,—
Something that reigns within thee,
Claiming utterance on every feature,
Motion, word of thy sweet life,—

Something that holds thee unapproachable;
Yet draws me ever nearer in unconsciousness,—
Something that makes thee, God, and me,
A fool; yet offers cheer, in that I
May deify myself in its far light,—

A mystic magnetism of Infinity !—
Thy soul, so full of good that when
I touch thy hand it thrills me through,
And lifts me into life !

THE OLD TEACHER.

OCTOBER reigned, and the golden wand
  Of autumn had waved above the wood,
Till she doffed her emerald garments bright,
  And rolled her form in the robes of blood.
On the beech, like ear-rings of coral, hung
  The crisp, red leaves, fantastic curled ;
While the slumbering spirit of glory dreamt
  Round nature's heart, and chained the world.
The air, like a halo of golden mist,
  Hung, dead, on the bosom of sorrowing earth ;
And the mute, soft lips of the river kissed
  The leaves, as they twirled from their airy berth.
The last wood-warbler caught the air ;
  And, wild and aloft on his venturous wing,
Rang out wild notes of the dying year,
  Then passed away to the land of spring ;
While his mellow cadences, one by one,
  Fell soft from the cloudless realms of sky,
As if some sweet angel, to breathe a prayer,
  Had swept through the pearly gates on high.
The world, in a dream between love and fear,
  Was hush'd in the tranquil of deep repose,
And life in the halcyon languish'd low ;
  Still, silent and dead lay the harp and the rose.
In this pangless death-dream, a sweet profound
  Opened its ports to the mind's swift tread ;
Till it caught a glimpse of eternal things,
  And the vale of wonder beyond the dead.

As, like setting stars, his companions sank,
   And the vigor of youth and life decayed.
But ever his faith grew strong, as he toiled
   Long and late for the promised goal;
Though betimes, in rage, the tempests broke,
   In their awful sweep, round his feeble soul.
And year by year, as his youthful band
   Passed out from the pale of his palsied sway,
To the world—to the world of might and men,
   With a tear, he said, "Work, watch, think, pray!"
But, back through the vista of rolling years,
   His mind now stole, till it reached the hour
When he first took charge of the old log school,
   In the primal glow of manhood's power.
And he thought of a glorious day, gone by,
   When he placed a bride on his heart's bright throne;
But two liquid pearls that fell from his eye
   Expressed, "Alas! I am left alone."
But yet, though resigned to his fate in life—
   For he knew some cross we had all to bear—
Deeply he mourned, that he had not toiled
   For his Master more when his hours were fair.
And thus he mused, "Though the voice of man
   Has never applauded or sounded my name;
Though, when this temple of earth dissolves,
   No tribute I give to the triumph of fame;
I heed not; but, oh, for the martyrized vows!
   Oh, for the moments of treasure misspent!
Oh, for the music and sunshine of heaven!
   That have breathèd, in vain, on my sinful content.
Oh, that the past, with its kingly grace,
   Would only revisit the portals of life!
How I'd hallow the precious dower of time,
   And win mankind from the lusts of strife!"

But the smiles of children gathered around;
   And a sweet "Good morn" from youth's light heart

Awakened his mind from its ancient dream,
   And the veiling of clouds was riven apart.
Then the old school-bell went toll, toll, toll,
   With the changeless throb of a hundred years,
While the children moved to its measured roll,
   Like the glad roll-call of the gliding spheres.

On the walls depended four mottoes old,
   Carved and gilt by the master's hand—
On the east was, "Seek the Morning Light,
   For it heralds the brink of the bordering land."
On the west, "Toil on! Toil on! Toil on!
   For the night soon comes when man cannot work."
On the north, "Be Firm! Be Brave! Be Strong!"
   On the south, "The Christ, the Cross, and the Ark."

The rosy light of the autumn morn
   Poured soft and sweet on his tresses gray;
As the teacher clasped his hands, thin-worn,
   And whispered low, "Let us kneel and pray."
And the whisper, echoing sweetly, swelled
   Down through the desks, as the voice of love;
And the angels silenced their blessed wings,
   To hear the words of that prayer above.

But the trembling dust, before his God,
   Scarce deigned to open the faltering lip;
For he saw the fountains of glory rise,
   And his soul was athirst, yet he dare not sip.
Now, higher and sweeter the murmurs grew,
   Bursting in eloquence bold at length,
As the voiceless roll of the deep sea-wave
   Breaks from the blue profound in strength.

"Father in heaven, oh, hear our prayer!
   Humbled for mercy, before Thee we bend;

Thou art our God immutable, wise;
   Grace and redemption to each of us send!
Oh, we adore Thy omnipotence, Lord!
   Jehovah, we bless Thy immaculate Son!
Prostrate, repentant, before Thee we fall;
   What have we done for Thee? What have I done?"
The prayer ceased; but the spirit wing'd,
   Hoping and trembling, up to the throne;
And the deep blue sky, to the gates of heav'n,
   And the stars rejoiced, and the mighty sun.

And the Savior pronounced his glad "Well done,
   Thou servant, faithful, good, and true!
Thou hast finished thy course, thou hast kept thy faith,
   Henceforth there's a crown in heaven for you!"

Then the Savior pointed him down to earth,
   Where the planet rolled through the light of heaven;
And the legion sons of the old log school
   To the farthest shores of the earth were driven.
And the fruit of his toil was surpassingly grand,
   For the seeds that were scattered in doubting and pain
Had taken deep root, and flourished the heart,
   And the hundred-fold was planted again.

He saw, where the desert of glittering sands
   Its bosom upheaved to the monarch of day,
The army of mercy unfurling its flag,
   And his lost boy marshalled the grand array.
And, here and there, in a pulpit rose,
   From his dear old boys, the rapturous roll;
While the eye aglow, and the hectic brow,
   Pronounced the eloquence deep of the soul.
And floating away on the wings of time,
   His precepts were speeding with healing and might;
For the cry and the soul of each earnest prayer
   Was the counsellor's motto, "Seek the Light!"

He beheld, in the great school-halls of earth,
    Where Genius and Learning sat throned in their pride
In the empire of wisdom, his sons holding sway,
    Proclaiming the truth to the universe wide;
Till knowledge and light resplendent prevailed,
    Where earth and her children were groping in dark,
As the sons of the old log cottage ruled,
    Saying, "Take refuge in Wisdom's Ark."

The deep, dark ocean rolled and heaved,
    While its tortuous billows leaped in mirth,
As the loud winds howled in their angry strength,
    And the thunder glared on the shuddering earth;
And the sea-king reeled on his dizzy path,
    And shot like a dragon from wave to wave;
But the teacher heard a well-known voice
    Bid his men, "Be Strong! be Firm! be Brave!"

He next beheld the groaning forge,
    With its red sons laid on its mighty breast—
The white stars shot from their molten ire,
    When the great sledge rang on their glowing crest.
Lo! the tiny hands, he had taught to write,
    Had grown to those pillars of bone and brawn;
And they made the giant anvil ring,
    As they sang, "Toil on! Toil on! Toil on!"

Then the sons of morning shouted for joy,
    "Well done! well done!" and the vault of heaven,
Swelled with the rapturous glory, rang,
    As the incorruptible crown was given;
And the teacher sat in his royal robes,
    Heaven's new-found joy in his jubilant soul;
While the children gazed on his pallid face,
    And the old school-bell went toll, toll, toll.

THE SONG OF ROBBIE BURNS.

What song does the peasant sing,
    As he turns the furrows long,
'Neath the blue, blue sky of Spring,
    All the birds and flowers among ?
'Tis the song of the heart in joy ;
'Tis the song of a glorious boy ;—
    The world, as around it turns,
    Sings the song of Robbie Burns !

What song can awake the soul
    To feel rich in its misery,
Inspiring a loftier hope,
    Than the eyes of earth can see ?
'Tis the song of woe resigned ;
'Tis the voice of a glorious mind ;
    The world, as around it turns,
    Sings the song of Robbie Burns !

What song can dissolve the ice,
    And the winter-drifts of grief,
Transpiercing the prison-walls
    With a radiant warm relief ?
'Tis the bird of the love-blent wing,
In his song of eternal spring ;—
    The world as around it turns
    Sings the song of Robbie Burns ?

What song has the lyrist, Love,
    Effused to the zephyr-sigh,
Wooing and capturing hearts
    With its artless melody ?
'Tis the song of Genius' heir ;
'Tis the song of the bard of Ayr ;—
    The world as around it turns,
    Sings the song of Robbie Burns !

What song makes nations rise
   In the might of the mighty free,
Spurning the tyrant's chains
   Marching on to Liberty ?
'Tis the song of the peasant sage ;
'Tis the song of the coming age ;
'Tis the song of a prince's soul ;—
'Tis freedom's chariot-roll ;—
   The world, as around it turns,
   Sings the song of Robbie Burns !

IT MAY NOT BE.

It may not be, that, in supreme communion,
   Upon Love's throne, our hearts may ever reign,—
That, in the bliss of infinite reunion,
   Our Hopes and Faiths may grow to golden grain ;—
This may not be ; and yet, I love thee.

It may not be, that, in thy radiant vision,
   My raptured eyes shall fathom constantly,
And meet the ocean-deep, soul-quieting decision
   That makes me live, and live alone for thee ;—
This may not be ; and yet, I love thee.

It may not be, that, in cool, soft entwining,
   Thy hands may soothe my palpitating brow,—
Or, that thy gracious words, in my repining,
   Shall cheer my fearful hopes to life, as now ;—
This may not be ; and yet, I love thee.

It may not be, that, ever blessing, guarding,
   Ennobling my purposes and aims,
Thou shalt be near to know my heart's rewarding,
   Or share a bounty which thy loving claims ;—
This may not be ; and yet, I love thee.

But I have wreath'd in flowers that never perish,—
    And graved on walls impervious to decay,—
Wove, in my soul, thy image,—*This* I'll cherish,
    Since we must part, when thou art far away;—
This—this may be; and so I love thee!

THE LIGHT, THE TRUTH, THE WAY.

When darkness shrouds the sun of love,
    And bathes the soul in tears;
When, lost upon the rolling flood,
    The bark of life appears;
Thy promise, bursting on the sight,
    Speaks soothingly,—" I am the Light."

When, o'er the golden gates of morn,
    The blinding vail of vice is thrown;
And the young heart, with aching beat,
    Is left to dare the gloom alone;
How welcome to despairing youth
    Thy promise bright,—" I am the Truth"!

When friendship false sweet hope betrays,
    And chronic doubt corrodes the faith;
When Mercy vails her blessed eye,
    Nor lights the pilgrim-step from death;
How precious, at Destruction's Bay,
    These Saviour words "I am the Way"!

A THOUGHT.

    When, traveller, night
Doth hold thee in its dark embrace, and sin

Doth make despair fill all thy soul, because
Thou art in darkness, seek the light! Survey,
Consider, pause; and, surely thou shalt find,
In darkest, deepest vale, some beacon-star.
Turn thou and follow.
     Though it lead thee far
From thy intended way, yet it doth shine
From heaven; there will it lead.

BATTLE HYMN.

Ye sons of Canada, awake!
 The star of morn has left the sky;
 Your fathers' flag of victory,—
 That glorious banner floats on high,
 Earth is beneath and God above;
 And human life is heavenly love;
 Arise, young legions, onward move!
Oh sons of Canada, awake!

Ye sons of Canada, awake!
 The sway of Ignorance is past;
 Wisdom supremely rules at last:
 Come forth and share the battle feast;
 Nor let the march of other nations
 Surpass your glory and your stations,
 In Knowledge, Science, Art's relations,
Oh sons of Canada, awake.

Ye sons of Canada, awake!
 The stranger's heart is dark with war;
 The muffled triumph beats afar;
 And filled with heralds is the air;
 Though tyrants rule your social wave,
 Yet Glory's sleeping in the grave;

BATTLE HYMN.

    Smite, smite them down ! your country save !
Oh sons of Canada, awake !

Ye sons of Canada, awake !
    Protect the rights your sires have won !
    The heritage of sire to son,—
    The crown of Peace,—Hope's rising sun.
    'Tis valor to adore the light ;
    'Tis honor to make free with might ;
    'Tis glory to establish right !
Oh sons of Canada, awake !

Ye sons of Canada, awake !
    Stretch forth the mighty arm of toil ;
    Embattle, beautify the soil
    Your fathers won by brave turmoil ;
    And, while your glory swells, behold
    Your virgin empire still unfold
    Her halcyon hope, her wealth untold,—
Oh sons of Canada, awake !

Ye sons of Canada, awake !
    Let Christian mercy shrine your heart ;
    Let vice and vanity depart ;
    The poor may fight their country's part ;—
    Extend the hand of brotherhood
    To honest hearts and loyal blood,—
    The truly brave are truly good !
Oh sons of Canada, awake !

Ye sons of Canada, awake !
    While, in your loyal bosoms, burns
    The patriot's fire, the heart that warns,
    That victory loves, that thraldom spurns,—
    Bid those, who would oppress you, know
    You dread not death, you fear no foe ;—
    Your swords are sharp, your bosoms true !
Oh sons of Canada, awake !

Ye sons of Canada, awake!
  Behold the grass on which ye tread,
  Behold the white stars overhead,
  All labor for a common need :—
  'Tis sacred dust beneath your feet;
  Your fathers' graves! in memory sweet,
  Their patriot spirits ever beat!
Oh sons of Canada, awake!

IN VAIN.

I.

Why do you linger 'mid the shadows,
  Evening's dew upon thy brow;
Why is Hope thus sadly dreaming,
  Clothing thy warm smiles in snow;
Why has night's unfathomed deadness
Clouded all thy morning gladness,
In a spell of never ending,
In a vision Life transcending?

Would you know the sullen angel,
  Shrouding Love's twilight in pain;
This the spell,—oh, this the vision;
  I have loved, and loved in vain!

II.

Have sweet Friendship's loyal greeting,
  Smiles of joy, and cheering word,
Love's warm raptured strong devotion,
  Breathing rose or trilling bird,
Not some power of glad alluring,
From the loveless clouds obscuring?

Can the sun's majestic glory,
Not renew love's artless story ?

Ne'er can these dissolve the shadows,
   That eternally remain ;
For my heart is dead and buried,—
   I have loved and loved in vain !

III.

Come and join our happy sallies ;
   Dance and sing thy grief away ;
Hide in rose-embowering valleys,
   Till the angel loses thee !
Then, oh, then, our glad old greetings,
Shall relume our mirthful meetings !
On thy lips, blest love shall tremble ;
In thy heart, bright hopes assemble.

Can the withered leaf of autumn
   Yet reclaim its verdure bright ?
Can the Sun's imperial fingers
   E'er unweave the veil of night ?
Once this heart knew Love's warm magic
   Ne'er to feel that thrill again ;
For my life is wound in shadows ;—
   I have loved and loved in vain !

LOYALTY AND WAR.

BRITANNIA, sceptered empress of the world !
Around whose royal throne, the loud acclaim
Of universal joy is never wing'd
With less than victory ! The nations all,
As subjects to a queen, before thee bow.

O'er all the earth, thy wide domain extends ;
Or where stern Thulè, priding in his power,
Breathes winter on the blast, and sepulchres
The vasty deep in adamantine chains ;
Or where the torrid sun his golden rain
Quivers among the palm-groves of the South,
And from his lofty throne commands the sea
To mount on airy wings and form on high ;
Where winter holds eternal court ; or where
Ithurial glory plays on every breeze,
And Hebe's bloom on Nature's cheek remains ;
Where Roman flag has ne'er been taught to sweep,
Nor Macedonian hero quaffed the cup
Of amber fame,—where Persian sceptre, crown'd
With Ophir gold, has ne'er been swayed,—Behold !
There floats the flag triumphant o'er the world,
Dishonored never by the stain of shame,—
The flag that never fell, while British blood,
In British hearts remained beneath its shade,—
The flag that rules the azure wave, and links,
In sympathy, the universe of mind,—
The lion-guarded flag of Britain !

       Thought,
When its rapt eye surveys thy wide domain,
Earth-circling, glorious and humane, arise,
And spread its magic pinions round the world,
Wisdom its watchword, and its motto Truth,
With patriotic ardor swells the heart ;
Strikes every nerve with animating thrill ;
And robes the past more georgeously than spring,
Than fancy more enrapturing.

      How dear
To us is every arpent of thy realm,
Britannia ! The blood that quickens in our veins,
And beats with fiery ardor in our hearts,—

That blood was shed for thee!—our fathers' blood!
The stars, that light thy empire from the dome
Of heaven, but count the legions of our sires
Who conquered Death by Victory. Th' altars
Of thy fame are fed with sacrifice; them
The glory of their dying breath incensed.
We till, in peace, our fathers' battle-fields;
Their blood still sanctifies our native soil;
Still, in the song of the dark forest glade
We hear their shouts of triumph. Our bright streams,
While rushing to the sea, discourse to us
The deathless lustre of the mighty dead.
We are their sons. We guard their sacred graves;
Can we their worth forget? No; save in sleep;
Nor yet in sleep, for every dream's low voice
Is hallowed by the thrilling touch of memory,
And yet, there are within Kanatia's homes,
Who such indictments urge,—disloyalty
And shame upon their heads! Themselves removed
From loyalty, and disavowing all
That constitutes true worth and dignity,
Clinging to shattered vestiges of hope,—
The shadow of a shadow,—scanning all
From out the narrow kingdom of their minds,
They deem all men alike.

     The man, who would
Not guard the temples of his sires; nor count
It victory to die for them;—to shed
His blood in rev'rence of the memory
Of such as bought his hope with theirs;—who would
Not kindle to a patriot's fire, to see
A stain upon his country's fame,—he is
Unworthy of a soldier's death; nor should
His ashes find a resting-place, among
The honored dust of heroes nobly born,
Or martyrs gloriously slain.

And yet
Thy pride, Britannia, springs not from thy wars;
Nor do thy sons esteem no glory save
The blood-dyed sabre and the battle-field,
With vanquished fellowmen heaped slain; there is
A flame of filial love in British hearts,
That makes them *feel* as well as *act*. They smite,
In vengeance dread, their country's foe; then weep
O'er his brave fall in nobler tears than Love's.
The wondrous excellence and brilliancy
Of thy most honored and exalted name
Bursts not in mad ambition from its source,
Like lurid lava from Vesuvius' throat;
But, like the stately and majestic flow
Of some grand stream, it sweeps, in grace,
From pure recesses of that mount sublime
Of Contemplation and long-nurtured love,
Heaped by true, steady and untiring hands
And hearts of Britain's Great and Good and True!
With heaven-inspirèd heart and hand humane,
From civil bondage and from social vice
Thou hast reclaimed the fallen sons of men;
And snatched, of slavery, the cursed chains
From off the servient neck of the swart sons
Of Ethopia. Thou hast endowed
The natives of thy farthest isle with name—
The noblest under heav'n,—the name of Man.
Upon the shackle-chafèd hand, thou'st plac'd
The token of immortal Freedom's sons;
And sent the fetter-freighted feet to run
On works of liberty and love. And where
Revolting Passion and the bestial bane
Of thraldom furrowed, deep, with hellish share,
The god-like brow of Beauty, Youth and Age,
There inborn Freedom hath resumed her throne,
And, olive-crowned, holds sway imperial.
But paramount o'er all thy great reforms

Stands that which heralds to idol'trous shore,
Remote from every source of joy, the light,
Supernal beaming from the Cross,—that Light
That bursts asunder love-obscuring clouds.
And, on the brow of Night, sets Morning's Star,—
That steals like warm, sweet, soft, impulsive throb
Of new-born Hope ; till rising to a true
And perfect life, it unthrones sin ; destroys
The cruel thirst of earthly lust ; implants
And nurtures Charity in human hearts ;
Saves, glorifies the Soul.

     But strange it seems
Britannia, that the heart, that succors pain,
Should wield the arm that sows distress and death !
Behold, afar in Afric's burning clime !
See yon bright galaxy of Christian men
Breathe gospel radiance to the dark-brow'd throng,
Their banner blazon'd with Salvation, Love,
The Cross, the Crown !—these are the Mission Knights ;
And Britain's sons across her earth-wide realm
God-speed the heroes of the Cross ; and give
The cause of Life and Peace, their toil-won gold.

But look again ; on yon far, lofty hill
That rears its purple crown amidst the glow
Of evening splendor on the horizon limned,
Behold yon black, disastrous, death-like cloud
Sweeping its volume o'er the golden crest.
Hear, hear the long-protracted thunder roll,
As iry Vulcan, from his black abode,
Had roused the vengeance of his myriad sons,
These, too, are Britain's sons,—their mission, *death*,
That thickening cloud the martial field-array,
This horrid roar the voice of cannonade,
Britannia's flag ! Britannia's heraldry !
Victory, Empire, Glory, Sword and Shield !

Forward they march, the bannered legions brave !
Brave, glorious hearts in an inglorious cause ;
And now, along yon mountain's shadowy side,
The hovering smoke-clouds having swept away,
A scene of horror meets the startled gaze,
The strangely-clad, but royal-hearted black,
Lie thick, in carnage, on their native haunts,
Their banners reeking in their warriors' blood,
With here and there a deathless dying chief
Still clutching, in his freezing grasp, the red
And fatal assagai. The peaceful towns,
Where Industry, though rude, was cherished still,
Now stretch one long and level plain of hot
And bitter desolation. In the homes,
Where beamed the smiles of mirth and innocence,
Now wrack the whirlwind's of Despair and Woe.

The roar of battle has delayed ; and from
The wilding warfare of dark Zululand ;
The sons of battle are recalled to share
A nation's gratitude and sovereign's smiles,
Rejoicing cities spread the battle-feast ;
And bid their thousand bells peal ardently
Their brazen throbs ; and leaping bonfires shoot
Their hungry pallid breath on high ; until
The soft, blue sky stoop reverently and catch
The ascending essence as an incense smoke.
And up beneath the proudly mottoed arch,
In one long, winding, surging, struggling stream,
Their bosoms swelling with the breath of fame,
With Glory's royal flame their eyes aglow,
And steps in time with music's stately march,
The soldier-sons, the lion-warriors march.
Along the lines, the mounted marshals fly ;
The gallant chargers fiery, fierce and fleet,
Wheel angry crescents, spurn the yielding earth.
The foamy wrath, the bursting veins, red eye ;

The arching neck, clear nostrils quivering wide ;
The war-dance wild, the vengeful neigh,—all say
They've shared the battle-shock ; the glory too
Shall share. Forward they march, until they gain,
The precincts of yon amphitheatre,
The long, long lines are formed in martial mass.
Then, while a thousand waxen stars illume
The scene, and break coruscant on the crests
And blazoned shields, a thousand thousand songs
Proclaim the proud hurrah of British fame ;
Sovereign, Princes, Poets, Statesmen, Wits,
Arising, swell the volume of applause ;
Bestow the Cross of Honor, and the Star
Of fame on valiant breasts and noble brows :
While, ever and anon, th' approving shout
Rises in pæans from th' assembled throng,
And little boys are dancing all around,
Madly in joy, and wishing they were men,
All—all is joy ! ah, no ! for, in a deep
And melancholy undertone of woe,—
A weeping soul that cannot find a tongue—
A death-like groan prolonged and wild you hear ;
And, struggling into higher life, at last
It bursts, a cry ! What then ? Ah ! you behold
A host of lovely virgins on a hill,
In awful anguish wringing of their hands,
Vainly assaying to command their hearts,
A brother dear or heart betrothed is gone !
For ever, ever gone ! All—all this world
Is dark and drear on their fair, loving lives ;
Their hopes forever dead. There, too, observe
Yon aged mother, wretched and decayed,
Sitting alone in tattered garments old,
Her snow-white hair clouding a feeble brow,—
Her riven heart can barely summon strength
To say in tears, between the sobs,—"Oh God !
My son ! my only stay ! my darling son !"

You turn, in sorrow, wonder, from the sight,
And pain supplants the mounting flame of joy.
You then perceive, along the stony streets,
Cold, naked feet of little ragged boys,
And darling blue-eyed little girls, who should
Be angels of some cheerful hearth; and when
They see you come, the famished, pinched lips
Affect a painful smile, the tiny heart
Beats for a moment warm; and, as you pass,
In dread of wrath, you hear them whisper, "Bread"!
You pause amazed; and, to suppress the tear,
Enquire the cause. The answer comes:—" Alas
Good, loving fathers had we once; but they
Have fought and fell in Zululand; and we
Are forced to beg."
     Of Zululand you think,—
Think of the gory battle-field, the host
Of slaughtered warriors, widowed mothers poor,
And tawny babes that prattle of dead sires.
Then stand with me and curse the demon War,
That spreads, on smiling lands, such direful scenes;
Destroys the budding hopes of fair, young hearts;
And leaves our British blood to nourish soil
Ne'er to be ours. Oh! for a Wilberforce,
Whose noble, philanthropic, godly life
Would consecrate itself to this grand cause
Of human liberty and human right,
And conquer! Onward roll, thou mighty stream
Of Knowledge, Wisdom, Peace! Roll on! and spread
Thy precious, healing waters o'er the earth,
Making mankind a common brotherhood;
Dispersing by thy golden beacon-light
The antiquated shades of Ignorance,
War, Passion, Slavery; until, at last,
The kingly throne of Reason be adored,
And men and nations dwell in Love and Peace.

TO A WOULD-BE SUICIDE..

Dull earth-begotten worm of pride!
Would'st thou creative love deride?
Ignoble monster! would'st thou hide
      Thy sin-scarred life from man;
And, shrouding sin in blood of death,
With guilt upon thy latest breath,
Meet High Omnipotence in wrath,
      And bear th' eternal ban?

The trodden grass, the dankest weed,
The meanest flower that, in the mead,
Rears over earth its dewy head,
      Rejoices in its life;
When beaten dead to cheerless earth,
It soon revives in second birth,
To live is its primordial worth,
      And triumph over strife.

Th' itinerant bird without a home,
The herds that, wild and wanton, roam
In woe and want, despise the tomb—
      In courage death defy.
Blest instinct tutors them to seek,
With tireless toil, and patience meek,
In lonely wood, by darkling creek,
      Their life. They *will* not die.

Yon servile dastard, willing slave,
Who, life to bondage, meanly gave;
Yon mendicants that morsels crave—
      Those are too brave to die.
Enduring cross, and suffering curse,
The pang of hunger, sin's remorse,

They summon soul, faith reinforce—
    Life is their victory !

Upon the golden scroll of fame,
Ten thousand heroes have a name,
That might have filled the tomb of shame,
    Were they unleal to life ;
But they have earned the victor-wreath,
Crown'd noble life with glorious death,
And, through war's thunder-cloud beneath,
    They soared beyond all strife.

Art thou a man ? can'st thou behold
Nature her galaxy unfold,
God's promises inscribed in gold,
    And not desire to live ?
Art thou beneath yon senseless plant,
Yon soulless brute, that knows by want,
Yon slaves that, like yoked oxen, pant ?
    If so, I thee forgive.

Is thy life nothing ? selfish slave,
To drop it in the laughing wave !
Christ died that very life to save,
    That thou wouldst spurn from thee !
Oh, how wouldst thou before Him stand,
With His, thy blood upon thy hand,
When He the treasure will demand,
    Upon the Judgment Day ?

Life is so precious, that, to run
The chance of it from peril won,
A thousand have been lost for one ;
    Nor lost in vain were 'they ;
For living true was ne'er in vain,
Nor living, dying falsely, gain,

TO A WOULD-BE SUICIDE.

Truth may an hour in sleep remain,
    But lives eternally.

Yon palpitating spheres of light,
Haunting the dreams profound of night,
Behold them dance in cycles bright!
    Behold the king of day
Scaling the azure mount! how blest!
Oh, man! believe, within thy breast,
Nobler than all combined—the best,
    Thy royal life doth stay.

Art thou, on earth, without *one* friend,
Hopeless, weak, joyless, poor, disdained,
Outcast, dejected, malice-stained?
    This is the cry of all!
The king upon the purple throne;
The beggar starving on a stone;
Man! *this* is life, and *this* alone—
    To triumph, not to fall!

Who'd live, while yet untried his steel?
Who'd fear to mount, to fight, to feel?
Life is but sifting out the real
    From tinsel and deceit.
Who best can bear the heaviest weight,
And falters most with wily fate
Lives most, lives best,—he, he is *great*
    Most recompense shall meet.

Look up, my friend, for from above,
There comes a magic flow of love
Bidding the soul love's power approve,
    Showing the perfect path.
There is one Friend who never failed;
There is one Star that never paled;

There is thy God who never railed
    On penitence and faith.

Confide, my brother, in mankind
Midst passion, sorrow, gropings blind ;
All are like thee—no human mind
    But feels for human woe.
From self, look out into the sea
Of human action ; and be free
In sympathy with misery
    And soon thy cup will overflow.

THE END.

www.ingramcontent.com/pod-product-compliance
Lightning Source LLC
Chambersburg PA
CBHW020253170426
43202CB00008B/343